Befriending God touched [...]
know God in a way that [...]
friendship. As I turned e[...]
the next line would offer, Tanya's heartfelt stories and biblical
insight would often cause me to pause. This is not a book to
be rushed but savored. Every chapter is rich and deep and
hopeful for anyone who thinks they are too insignificant to
make a difference. If you are tired of seeing God as distant or
demanding and you are ready to know more deeply the God
who sees you, then run, don't walk, to get this book!

Karrie Scott Garcia, founder of Freedom Movement, author of
Free and Fully Alive, and international speaker

Tanya Godsey's work at the intersection of spiritual formation
and worship makes her an ideal guide to finding freedom and
connection with our Creator. Her journey through suffering,
disruption, and complexity equips her with the wisdom to
navigate life's challenges.

Rev. Sandra María Van Opstal, author of *The Next Worship*

Every word in this book is intentional, flows from the secret
place, and holds wisdom from the woundings God has redeemed
in Tanya's story. It carries an invitation to journey the narrow
road that leads to true life. It will cost you everything to
accept this invitation, but the reward is an abiding life of love,
friendship, and purpose. Come all who are homesick, outcast,
burdened, and lonely, and find your true home in God Himself.

Tori Mae Hein, freedom coach and director of marketing for
Freedom Movement

In a time when life often feels disenchanted and full of wandering, Tanya's words walk us home to the heart of God. Her use of story, both biblical and personal, invites us to experience an intimate friendship with God in our own lives. *Befriending God* is filled with wisdom, wonder, and direction.

Hannah Wood, Redeeming the Story board of directors

BEFRIENDING GOD

How We Are
Undone,
Changed,
and
Made New

TANYA GODSEY

A NavPress resource published in alliance
with Tyndale House Publishers

NavPress.com

Befriending God: How We Are Undone, Changed, and Made New

Copyright © 2025 by Tanya Gilmore. All rights reserved.

A NavPress resource published in alliance with Tyndale House Publishers

NavPress and the NavPress logo are registered trademarks of NavPress, The Navigators, Colorado Springs, CO. *Tyndale* is a registered trademark of Tyndale House Ministries. Absence of ® in connection with marks of NavPress or other parties does not indicate an absence of registration of those marks.

The Team:
David Zimmerman, Publisher; Deborah Sáenz, Editor; Elizabeth Schroll, Copyeditor; Olivia Eldredge, Managing Editor; Libby Dykstra, Designer; Sarah K. Johnson, Proofreading Coordinator

Cover illustration of burning bush copyright © by Marina/Adobe Stock. All rights reserved.

Cover photograph of gold texture copyright © by kyoshino/iStockphoto. All rights reserved.

Author photo copyright © 2023 by Jacob Gilmore. All rights reserved.

Published in association with The Bindery Agency, TheBinderyAgency.com

Some of the anecdotal illustrations in this book are true to life and are included with the permission of the persons involved. All other illustrations are composites of real situations, and any resemblance to people living or dead is purely coincidental.

For information about special discounts for bulk purchases, please contact Tyndale House Publishers at csresponse@tyndale.com, or call 1-855-277-9400.

ISBN 978-1-64158-867-6

Printed in the United States of America

31	30	29	28	27	26	25
7	6	5	4	3	2	1

Father, Spirit, Son, Three in One,
I've got my whole world in three persons.

CONTENTS

INTRODUCTION

God Is Our Permanent Home

The moment we open our eyes in this post-Eden world, we encounter certain realities. None of us choose where we are born, whom we are born to, and what we are born with (or without). From day one we are each given a certain set of internal and external variables entirely beyond our control: the color of our skin, the presence or absence of a stable family system, the inclusion or exclusion of God in daily living, and the socioeconomic status of our household, just to name a few. As we draw our first breath, we do so in a world that has developed its own fallible systems around the acceptance or rejection of the variables we were born with and had no power to choose. We find ourselves at the mercy of a story we didn't opt into and in a cultural framework where this story makes us either likely or unlikely to flourish in the world. As time passes, we become increasingly fluent in the language of homesickness. Life on planet Earth is far from the perfection of Eden, and we can feel the effects of exile in our bones. We know life isn't supposed to be this way. We long to fill our lungs with the oxygen of home.

Sometimes I close my eyes and imagine Eden: the freshly created imagination of God embodied in a perfect garden, the astounding visuals in a newly created spectrum of color, the freshly born aroma of a new Earth, and the rushing river that watered it all. I imagine the soundscape of our original home, when echoes of a new song rang out in a new world and there was no barrier to original love, original design, and original relationship. What did it feel like when the earth exuded glory from sunrise to sunset? Sometimes I wonder what it felt like to be at the start of a story so pure and unstained. Our beginning, written into life by the Original Artist, the first to make something beautiful out of absolutely nothing. The One who was and is and is to come (see Revelation 1:8), the Love who is in all things and from whom all things came to life.

Sometimes I close my eyes and imagine the unhindered love and glory of our original home, and the wonder of it all washes over me like the wild blue mist of a waterfall or the glow of a golden sunset peeking over the Santa Monica Mountains. I remember we were all made from love and for love. We can feel it in the marrow of who we are. We know we were created for so much more and yet we live, move, and breathe in the tension of the *now* and *not yet*, where our longing for home lives somewhere in between the complexity of our post-Eden experiences and our beloved cotton candy sunsets. But what makes home . . . home? I've always believed home is less about the comforts around you and more about who opens the door to welcome you inside and who holds you close once you're there. And so what makes exile a tragedy is not a change of scenery but a change in intimacy, the ache of separation. At the heart of spiritual homesickness is the sting of relational distance and our yearning for wholeness with God as a person.

My earliest memories include having a deep sense that God Himself was the only true home I would ever know. Perhaps for me, the longing was born out of mounting deposits of feeling "too different to make a difference" as a little brown girl in an immigrant community. Perhaps it was a childhood spent witnessing the plight of a people who were born into a story they didn't choose with variables society used to dismiss them as damaged goods or bodies only worthy of less-than-minimum-wage work in the hot Texas heat. Roofers in 110-degree heat. Migrant workers covering their entire bodies with clothing for protection from the blazing sun. Women working tirelessly to make food to sell so they could buy food to eat. Weeks when my father, the pastor, was paid for shepherding an entire at-risk community. Weeks when he went without pay. Every day an accumulation, on a soul level, of *It's not supposed to be this way*. A longing for Eden. A longing for home. A longing for justice, mercy, and compassion for the last and the least. Perhaps it was the result of a lifetime of watching family members lay themselves on the altar of this cause. How could we not? The need was too great. The stories too heartbreaking. The faces too familiar. The bills too heavy to pay. The lost souls too important to look away from.

I believe innocence isn't just something you lose by firsthand, lived experience. Innocence is lost in knowing, seeing, and feeling too much. Some children were raised with bats and balls and board games. Some of us were raised to save the world. I grew up with a sense that the gospel had chosen me, and I knew it in my bones before I knew anything else. My mom has a picture of me that she has always treasured—I am eighteen months old in a yellow dress. Gold necklace. Pigtails. My hand is loosely holding a croquet mallet, and my eyes are staring into the camera as if I could see through the world . . . because, in fact, I could.

When I look at the photo of the little brown girl in the yellow dress, I can see my line of sight included realities I was far too young to understand.

As a pastor's daughter raised in a Mexican immigrant community, I was immersed in a culture that was beautifully interdependent but socioeconomically disadvantaged. When the community you call home struggles for basic survival, you grow up fluent in the language of impossibility. You become deeply aware this world is dismally distant from God's original design. You are given the gift of second sight to see earthly systems as frameworks created with imperfect regard for the loving intent and design of a relationship-first God who cares for all.

Cultural context is an influential driver in how we process life and contribute our God-given voices to the world. So, as a living witness to the stories of marginalization around me, my heart was uniquely shaped by the experiences I observed in the immigrant community I was raised in. While I was born into American citizenship in the West Texas plains, in contrast to my immigrant community, I counted myself as one who stood in solidarity with the plight of the beautiful, humble people I came to know as family. And although my native tongue was English, I became much too fluent in the dialect of human suffering to resign myself to apathy. The soul-piercing pain of racism, the lack of financial opportunity, the barriers of English as a second language, the desperation that accompanies suffering—these are just a few realities our community was faced with regularly.

As years passed and my understanding of modern culture deepened, my observations led me to the conclusion that unless God Himself intervened, without money, power, or pedigree, I, along with those in my community, would likely never have the resources or opportunities to influence the world with our gifts for the greater good.

And before I knew anything about theology, social justice, or power dynamics, I somehow instinctively knew this reality could not mirror the heart of a God who created each person in His image with unique gifts and a story to tell. From my earliest moments, I longed for peace, provision, and harmony in a dissonant world, a world that discarded unlikely people born with variables working against them, like me and those in our community.

Despite my early sobriety toward (awareness of) the world's brokenness, I was given an unexpected gift. I somehow inherently believed God had His eye on our community, on me, because the last was first in His Kingdom. I couldn't understand it then, but being raised in this humble setting would become the doorway to a deeply personal journey of befriending God. My soul-level friendship with Him would give me the greatest treasure I could be given on this side of heaven: the safety, security, and belonging of finding and abiding in my one and only true home. Seeing God's relationship-first nature illustrated through the pages of Scripture reinforced my faith in the reality that God has a special place in His heart for the unlikely. I risked my heart on friendship with God based on the fathers and mothers of our faith who needed nothing more to live meaningful, purpose-filled lives in intimacy with Him and destiny through Him. And in moments when I feared the finality of the variables the world used to label me as unworthy, I would remember the kinship I felt with every person in the biblical narrative chronicled in this book.

From a young age I believed that whatever or whomever I put my confidence in would define me. So my confidence was in God Himself—and it continues to be. I am not a statistician, but I would venture to say that a little brown girl raised in a marginalized community might have very low odds of being perceived as having been born with the "right" variables to be granted a voice in the world. The fact that you are reading a book penned by someone like this is nothing short of a relationship-first God demonstrating His power to redeem a story.

No one would argue against the fact that we are all formed by the stories we are born into, and yet, when we befriend God, these stories become the wick that is lit to shine God's brightness in the dark room of a homesick world. There is no doubt Moses' upbringing in Egypt was preparation for his destiny to free God's people from Pharaoh's oppression. It's clear David's intimacy with God was cultivated in the solitude and silence of sheep pastures. There's no question John the Baptist's dependence on God was developed in the obscurity of a wilderness relationship. But ultimately the power that flowed through their lives to change the world was not cultural or circumstantial; it was relational and therefore providential. God befriended these men personally in the landscape of their stories to produce a depth of intimacy that fully formed their character and then changed the world.

I suspect it was no accident I was immersed in a community that allowed me to view the gospel through the lens of the immigrant and the stranger. I suspect there was providence behind becoming a pastor's daughter exposed to 3:00 a.m. crisis knocks on the door. I believe the sovereignty of God was at play because these were the experiences that shaped the lens through which I see the biblical narrative and the world. This is why I lie in bed at night thinking about people experiencing homelessness, those facing suicidal thoughts who need just one person to watch and pray with them for one more night, children orphaned by parents battling addiction. I am not a theologian. I am not the lead pastor of a well-known church. I am a little brown kid whose life was profoundly marked by the Father, the Son, and the Holy Spirit in a poor, marginalized immigrant community, in the company of mis hermanos y hermanas . . . in a hundred different community enchilada fundraisers, in one-hundred-degree sweltering heat as the paletero rung his bell when our five-hour, Spirit-filled services let out. In too many baby showers for unwed mothers raised in unstable homes and too many funerals for at-risk teenagers gone far before their time. A Trinitarian God met me on the back side of Avenue A in a small Texas town, and though I've been many places in the world since, this same God has become my one true, permanent home.

As we begin our journey together, I want to aim our hearts upward toward one important truth. You and I have a soul, a soul set on an eternal trajectory. In a world of transience, our souls are designed to dwell securely in our permanent home, the sanctum of a deeply personal friendship with God. Psalm 139 reveals that all human life begins underneath His gaze, as we are fearfully and wonderfully woven and spun. John 15:5 invites us to dwell in Him through Christ, the Everlasting Vine. John 14:2 reminds us, "My Father's house has many rooms; if that were not so, would I have told you that I am going there to prepare a place for you?" His presence is where we began, where we're invited to abide, and where we are going. Our wildest blessings and our light and momentary afflictions can and will be taken away from us, but God is the mountain who will not be moved. He is our permanent home, and the invitation into personal friendship with Him is the foundation of every word of this book, no matter which corner of the world you come from.

In the midst of stories we didn't choose, with a set of external and internal variables entirely beyond our control, I want to offer some truth and consolation: The story the world wants to use to dismiss us, the enemy wants to use to destroy us, and the flesh wants to use to discourage us is the same one God wants to use to draw us into deeper friendship with Him.

He is a God who can be trusted and a permanent home safe enough to settle into. I've always loved this description of God's attributes, and I invite you to gaze upon the wonder of His qualities as we stand on the precipice of knowing Him more deeply through the invitation of this book.

> God is an invisible, personal, and living Spirit, distinguished from all other spirits by several kinds of attributes: metaphysically, God is self-existent, eternal, and unchanging; intellectually, God is omniscient, faithful, and wise; ethically, God is just, merciful, and loving; emotionally, God detests evil, is long-suffering, and is compassionate; existentially, God is free, authentic, and omnipotent; relationally, God is transcendent in being, immanent universally in providential activity, and immanent with his people in redemptive activity.[1]

In the crucible of my origin story, a passion for befriending this God as a person was born. With my curious heart and artistic leanings, I prayed God would cultivate a gift within me to inspire the world with beauty and meaning and open timely doorways into His timeless truths. I believe this book is, in part, an answer to this prayer, and it is my hope that within the following chapters the divine reality of the relationship-first God of the Old and New Testaments will encounter you in an unprecedented way to usher you into a deeper friendship with Him than any you've dared to pray for. My prayer for you as you enter the journey of this book is Ephesians 3:14-21 (NKJV):

> For this reason I bow my knees to the Father of our Lord Jesus Christ, from whom the whole family in heaven and

earth is named, that He would grant you, according to the riches of His glory, to be strengthened with might through His Spirit in the inner man, that Christ may dwell in your hearts through faith; that you, being rooted and grounded in love, may be able to comprehend with all the saints what is the width and length and depth and height—to know the love of Christ which passes knowledge; that you may be filled with all the fullness of God.

Now to Him who is able to do exceedingly abundantly above all that we ask or think, according to the power that works in us, to Him be glory in the church by Christ Jesus to all generations, forever and ever. Amen.

A FAMILY FOUNDED ON THE IMPOSSIBLE

Trusting in God's Power

The year was 1983. I had not yet started kindergarten, but I remember the vinyl seats in my father's Cordoba and the hot seat belt wrapped around my sensitive skin. I remember days of windows down while the Eurythmics graced the airwaves with "Sweet Dreams (Are Made of This)." *Return of the Jedi* ruled the box office and Cabbage Patch dolls were the heart's desire of every little girl, including yours truly. This was the year our family moved from Fort Worth, Texas, to start a church in a burgeoning Mexican American immigrant community in Godley, Texas (population: three hundred souls).

In Hebrews 11:8, we read, "By faith Abraham, when called to go to a place he would later receive as his inheritance, obeyed and went, even though he did not know where he was going."

I am struck by this verse every time I read it. Abraham "obeyed and went" even though he did not have the road map. Abraham, originally known as Abram, is our introduction to Israel as a nation. Abraham and his wife Sarah are the unlikely patriarch and matriarch, respectively, of the family of God. Eventually God would invite Abraham into a life-changing moment to gaze into a sea of stars as He promised to make the impossible possible, but initially Abraham was not given a clear plan as to *how* he and his wife would birth a nation without the physical capability of bearing a child in their old age.

It has always been a wonder to me that God would build His family based on a story that unfolds at the intersection of human impossibility and God's manifest power. Impossibility surfaces when something cannot be realized due to inescapable realities present in the natural world. In other words, we find ourselves in impossible situations when natural laws stand as a barrier to a specific desired outcome. On this side of heaven, we are subject to limitations that hem us in on every side of the human experience—and sometimes we have to wait a long while, expectantly watching for God's power to be made manifest.

In the same way Abraham left his homeland (Ur) for the land the Lord, his God, would give him, my family left the familiar and answered a call to ministry in rural Texas with nothing more than what Abraham held in his heart: the sincerity and security of a real-time friendship with God.

There are several things you should know about the foundation God would build our family's calling upon in Godley, Texas. This was a town where human beings were the minority and dairy cattle the majority. And despite the town's name, this community was anything but godly. This was a small town steeped in discrimination. As a Hispanic family shepherding a community of immigrant workers, we would not be handed a warm welcome. We would not inherit a building with a baptistry, a pulpit, AC, or nice wooden pews. We would be invited to facilitate our first church services in a barn.

Now, this wasn't a barn you might see in a bridal magazine. It wasn't an air-conditioned wedding venue with hardwood floors and chandeliers. This was a hot, hay-filled, musty cattle barn. Like Abraham and Sarah and many of the fathers and mothers in the biblical narrative, we would be asked to cultivate a missional call with nothing more than childlike faith . . . and the presence of God Himself.

> By faith he made his home in the promised land like a
> stranger in a foreign country; he lived in tents, as did
> Isaac and Jacob, who were heirs with him of the same
> promise. For he was looking forward to the city with
> foundations, whose architect and builder is God.
> HEBREWS 11:9-10

We settled into a new city, like strangers in a foreign land, with a beginning salary of one hundred dollars a week. Our first "church service" took place in record Texas heat. And there I was, dressed in my Sunday best, pigtails and a smile, against the backdrop of meekness. The story you are born into has a way of marking you with the belief that your reality is everyone's reality. I thought this was the way everyone worshiped on a Sunday morning.

But one day, as my father's eyes overflowed with tears, I was awakened to the difference between our reality and that of the rest of the world. His words shot like an arrow through the hearts of everyone in the room. "I'm not going to leave this town, but I'm not coming back here," he said. "This is a barn for cows, not for people."

A tiny heart and a tiny brain could not fully process the entire weight of this sentence, but tears happen to be a universal language. Tears do not require interpretation. To be human is to know heartbreak when you see it. There was an understanding among us that required very few words. As image bearers of God, we—and our dignity—lived in the tension of all that could not be said.

We left the barn while the local Baptist church was dismissing from their own air-conditioned church services. They caught a glimpse of my dad soaked in sweat. He seized the moment to say, "You're not serious about having us here. I'm willing to meet, but not in a cow barn. It's wrong. These people are not cows—they're human beings."

With this statement the missions committee who had invited us to town accepted the unsustainability of our circumstances and the inhumanity of an animal barn as a hospitable venue. We were transitioned to a tiny room in the local civic center. This is when the fires of persecution began to burn with increasing heat.

The room was free to everyone but us. We were forced to pay rent for use of the facilities. As word about our new venue traveled, the townspeople began to spread false narratives about our cleanliness as a community, even though we made sure to leave the venue better than we found it. Then one day, during one of our regularly scheduled meeting times, we went to use the civic center . . . only to find that the locks had been changed. On this day we had church service out in the parking lot with forty people in the blazing Texas sun. Women and children were given shade under the trees. Dad preached that day without protection from the heat, both literally and metaphorically. Once again there was an understanding among us that required very few words.

The civic center tripled our rent, and we paid triple until the townspeople made it so difficult for us to continue meeting there that the local Baptist church offered us a side room as a reprieve. Then came the complaints from the members of this church. The fires of discrimination followed us wherever we met.

But instead of consuming us, these fires stoked the embers of a hunger for God present within our community. God blessed our little congregation with His presence and a solidarity that unified, connected, and comforted us. We didn't have much, but we had God and each other, and somehow, this seemed like more than enough. As our numbers grew, a kindhearted farmer offered two acres of land, right outside the city limits, for us to build our own church. As you can imagine, news like this traveled faster than lightning in the small town of Godley, Texas. Before we knew it, rumors of the townspeople not being in favor of a Mexican American church anywhere near them boomeranged back to us. We breathed the air of impossibility daily. Our lungs had become heavy from the pollution of contempt, hatred, and vitriol. How would we move forward surrounded by such animosity? Frequently, God speaks a call before He reveals the blueprint. We lived in the tension of this reality. We needed oxygen, and it was given to us.

The land for our proposed new church was donated, which gave us hope that we'd have a suitable place to worship without being persecuted. But our encouragement changed to dismay when the phone rang in the wee hours of the morning one night. We had finally raised five thousand dollars to build a fence on the property, and it had been destroyed—intentionally. Impossibility had never felt more final. But word of this vandalism spread, and major media news outlets began to flock to our small town to document the story. One of their featured interviews included a woman who was one of several at the helm of the persecution. She was filmed saying, "Mexicans are like the cows they milk; they don't have souls." The media also interviewed my dad, who explained that the church was a mission sponsored by the Anglo church in town. He explained that the building would further our evangelism and discipleship efforts. When asked how we would build it, my dad answered, "I don't know, but God does." Upon the destruction of the fence—an act the FBI called a terroristic threat—we were faced with raising funds to rebuild it. Major media outlets continued to cover the story, and the events that followed were a divinely inspired surprise in which God began to write possibility into a seemingly impossible situation.

People from the greater Dallas–Fort Worth metroplex began to call to offer support. The news headlines read along the lines of "Pastor Godsey Has Faith That God Will Supply to Build This Church." One major article was published in the *Baptist Standard*. Soon thereafter the pastor of the local Baptist church called to say, "You've got some mail, Pastor Godsey. It's from East Texas."

A retired Baptist woman had written: "Young man, I was reading the *Baptist Standard*. Apparently they're not that godly in Godley, Texas. I want to encourage you not to leave. God will supply your needs. I live on Social Security and this is all I have, but the gates of hell will not prevail." A one-dollar bill was enclosed. This was the sign we had prayed for. Even though we did not know where we were going, there was one star shining in our pitch-black sky.

The next letter was from a president emeritus of Dallas Baptist University with a five-thousand-dollar check inside. The next day a dentist from Cleburne, Texas, sent in three thousand dollars. We received two hundred dollars here, five hundred dollars there. When all was said and done, fifteen thousand dollars had come in. That was a significant amount of money in 1983. Then the owner of a large cement company called and donated nine truckloads of cement. "It's wrong, what they've done to you," he explained.

In 1983 hate-filled townspeople destroyed our property. They called our home and left death threats and vile messages. They knifed our vehicles. They cursed our church community, but we had our faces set in the direction of obedience. We believed in a city whose architect and builder was God Himself, and this sustained us in the heat of the battle.

Then, three years into my family's stay, the tensions came to a head as townspeople created a petition to prevent us from building our church. Members from all the churches in the town signed it. Sometimes obedience has to be its own reward, and we faced this possibility week after week. At our court hearing, the only person who came to support us was Pastor Gordon, lead pastor of the Anglo church that had initially supported our church. He and my father sat on one side. What seemed like the entire town sat on the other. The judge laid the groundwork for respect before the court was in session, then he announced the case: *Citizens of Godley, Texas v. Pastor Godsey and Primera Iglesia Bautista.*

The judge said, "I'm going to make a statement. The last time I looked at the Constitution, there's freedom of speech and religion. And if Hare Krishna wants to buy property in Godley, Texas, to build his church, he can do it. If Sun Myung Moon wants to buy his own property in Godley, Texas, to build his church, he can do it. And if Reverend Godsey and the people of Primera Iglesia Bautista want to build a church on their land in Godley, Texas, the gates of hell will not prevail against them."

Dad later told me that he wanted to shout and cry in response, but he had been advised to remain silent. The judge gave the file to the court clerk and said, "Go file this in file 13." He told the townspeople, "Not one curse word, or I will arrest you, and I better not hear about you threatening this family again."

The FBI was present in the room but God the Father, Jesus the Son, and the Holy Spirit were the true guests of honor. God Himself, who had been a witness to every tear, every fear, and every moment between our yes to Him and the finality of this closure. He was there in the beginning, when we did not know where we were going, and had faithfully led us by the hand to this moment in time. The architect and builder of our faith made the impossible possible.

As God would have it, our church—a beautiful brick-and-mortar building—was built, and it still stands to this day. Amid impossible persecution and impossible circumstances, God invited our family into the evidence of things we could not see (Hebrews 11:1). He invited us to believe beyond the reality of sustained oppression and weekly death threats and into a place where we would receive reprieve from our "enemies" and the gospel would prosper to the glory of God.

We learned many things through this season of impossibility. Two of these lessons I'd like to highlight are

1. impossible situations position us for intimacy with God and
2. we must rely on internal resources from God.

Impossible Situations Position Us for Intimacy with God

Many planks were laid on the foundation of my faith during this season of persecution as God proved His dominion over the natural limitations of His people. I learned that impossibility positions us for intimacy. It suffocates self-sufficiency and oxygenates our reliance on God's sufficiency. It invites us into humility, the gift that's also a doorway to all blessing. Ultimately impossibility reminds us we cannot save ourselves. We are a people who have always needed and will always need a Rescuer.

We draw closer to God as a personal source of supernatural endurance in the crucible of patience. We align ourselves with His vision as we accept our own limitations and follow the current of God's activity with heightened expectancy and availability.

When we are faced with impossible situations, we are invited to take risks and say yes to invitations . . . without knowing exactly where we are going. This kind of childlike faith often leads to forward movement fueled by the activity of God.

We Must Rely on Internal Resources from God

Impossible situations also teach us to rely on internal resources given by God, not external resources mined from human reasoning or strategy. I learned early on that access to external resources such as money and power do not make the impossible possible in a way that ripples into eternity. External resources are always subject to post-Eden realities and the unrighteous dispensation of little-*g* gods present in this post-Eden world. But the God of Abraham and Sarah, the God of Isaac, the Great I Am, the One who was and is and is to come lavishly dispenses the needed internal resources from His Spirit and His Word to bring His Kingdom here, through His people, on earth as it is in heaven. As our faith community faced significant persecution in a small Texas town, God was rewriting the story of impossibility over our lives, for our good and His glory.

Like Abraham and Sarah, who stood on the precipice of a promise without the means to bring it to pass, Godley taught us that in the absence of external resources God would provide an inner sanctum where we could receive the internal resources needed from Him. But—also like Abraham and Sarah—this process occurred within the fallibility of our own humanity. We endured sleepless nights. We wrestled with discouragement and fear. We longed for comforts of the past. We felt the ache of our own humanity in it all. Yet when God invites us into faith, He has every intention of overshadowing our weaknesses with His supernatural strength.

> By faith, even though Sarah herself was barren and
> [Abraham] was too old, he received the ability to
> procreate, because he regarded the one who had given
> the promise to be trustworthy. So in fact children were
> fathered by one man—and this one as good as dead—like
> the number of stars in the sky and like the innumerable
> grains of sand on the seashore.
>
> HEBREWS 11:11-12, NET

Sarah and Abraham were not able to produce the desired results through the external resources of physical ability or human strategy. Like many who are faced with impossible circumstances, Abraham and Sarah wrestled with control only to be humbled into dependence, the doorway to the internal resource of faith.

In the flames of persecution, my church community could not produce our own desired outcomes through institutional favor, man's approval, or a "do more, try harder" mentality.

Like Abraham and Sarah, we had to go through a process of spiritual transformation to learn how to yield to God's shepherding hand. Only then did we learn how to simply receive what was being given . . . in His timing and His way.

We learned to look for God's unforced gifts, gifts drawn from the sacred reservoir of deep waters that flowed from the ocean of a life deeply connected with Him. External resources often failed, but internal resources flowed from the minutes and hours and days and years in our history with God in a holy confluence where springs, rivers, and tributaries joined through the power of the Spirit to nourish the dry land of our souls in wilderness seasons. In this sacred space we were given the supernatural faith to believe that what is impossible for man is possible with God. Millennia after Abraham and Sarah, I believe with all my heart that the faith of our fathers and mothers is one that still holds true.

In impossible situations—

We receive faith imparted through God's Word and accumulated through the halls of our history with Him.

We receive the fruit of God's Spirit cultivated through a quantity of quality time with Him in the sanctum of prayer.

We are given the gifts of the Holy Spirit as spiritual empowerment for the good works God has prepared in advance for us to do (Ephesians 2:10). Such gifts (prophecy, teaching, leadership, and mercy, to name a few) are imparted by God. When we employ these spiritual gifts, God's supernatural power supersedes our natural abilities.

Though Abraham and Sarah were too old for a son, God spoke impossible provision into impossible neediness. He is the same God today.

Though Abraham and Sarah's flawed human intervention created the complex plot twist of Hagar giving birth to Ishmael, God wrote impossible redemption into inevitable failure because He is both providential *and* He responds to real-time situations. He is the same God today.

Despite his error, Abraham remained tethered to his infallible Source in a world of fallible resources, and God received him. He is still the same God today.

Abraham and Sarah's spiritual formation happened in the same place ours does: in the epicenter of our inner world as it quakes with the force of our own sinful nature and the tension of living in a homesick world. Ultimately Abraham and Sarah knew what we are invited to believe now, that the love of God is greater than these tensions because God Himself is the Reality of all realities.

> By faith Abraham, when he was tested, offered up Isaac. He had received the promises, yet he was ready to offer up his only son. God had told him, "Through Isaac descendants will carry on your name," and he reasoned that God could even raise him from the dead, and in a sense he received him back from there.
>
> HEBREWS 11:17-19, NET

When Abraham was asked to sacrifice his son, the very son he had been asked to trust God to miraculously provide, by faith he believed and trusted in God's heart so much that he was certain God could raise Isaac from the dead. Abraham's external resources were not enough in a moment like this. Human reasoning was irrelevant. Systems of control failed. But in this moment God gave Abraham what he truly needed: the internal resources to enter what author and speaker Brennan Manning has called "ruthless trust."[1]

Impossibility is a gift that ushers us away from conceptual faith and into relational trust. Impossible timing, impossible circumstances, an impossible call . . . in moments like these, we must make an appeal to a very personal God and ask for His supernatural intervention. Often the question isn't whether God is capable of this level of miraculous intervention. Often the question is whether we are willing to surrender our grown-up strategies, to retrace our steps back to a posture of childlike faith. This childlikeness stands in contrast to our culture's current, which leads us to plan our way out of the possibility of God's surprises, out of the flow of the level of intimacy available to us when we face the impossible with Him, side by side.

At face value, money, power, beauty, achievement, education, influence, and intellectual capability are not inherently evil. These variables can be stewarded in health and are not destructive until they become little-*g* gods we place our confidence in instead of God Himself. Fear is at the root of our reach for anything that captivates our hearts more than the Great I AM, and we live in a culture that perpetuates fear. Fear of rejection. Fear of failure. Fear of loss. The spectrum of human fears is vast and wide.

So we reach for control. We prefer systems that guarantee outcomes and formulas that offer foolproof results. We prefer to choose the most likely path to success and have a propensity to avoid the least likely at all costs, even if divinely prompted to do so. But biblical faith is less math and more mystery. Equations leave little room for what Mother Teresa referred to as "the hand of a writing God."[2] Who is the real captain of the ship when our systems of control are on a cultural form of autopilot? The biblical narrative proves that the fiery furnace of the impossible brings us to a level of intimacy in which we are accompanied by a Divine Power who will walk through the flames with us. Our hearts are molded by the heat of impossibility, and the ultimate result is that we are increasingly formed into the likeness of Christ.

For reasons known only within the confines of God's divine sovereignty, Abraham and Sarah were the first two people written into the lines of Jesus' family tree. These two obscure individuals, well past their prime and unlikely to conceive, were chosen to become the first mother and father in the family of God's people of faith. Why would God begin the story of His covenant relationship with us through two people the world would dismiss? The biblical narrative is teeming with reminders that God's choice is frequently not man's choice. God's Kingdom is an upside-down Kingdom where the last is first and the first is last. God's choice will be accompanied by God's provision, and His choice will result in His glory, not man's.

Like each one of us, Abraham and Sarah were written into a story they didn't choose. They were invited into an untimely call and a dream they couldn't understand. Yet they were recipients of a promise: "In your offspring shall all the nations of the earth be blessed, because you have obeyed my voice" (Genesis 22:18, ESV). God's rescue plan for humanity took place through two unlikely people plucked out of obscurity.

Hebrews 11:1 tells us that "faith is the substance of things hoped for, the evidence of things not seen" (NKJV). Much like our call to Godley, Texas, God's invitation would mark the end of Abraham and Sarah's understanding and signal the beginning of a very personal undoing. The undoing—this happens to be where God does some of His best work.

Perhaps the time is right for a biblically informed undoing. While cultural Christianity in the West may statistically be on the decline in numbers, there's never been more of a palpable longing among God's people for the God of the Old and New Testaments to reveal Himself, in real time, in a profoundly personal, intimate, and unmistakably divine way. We want encounter. We want relationship. We want to *know* God, and we want to be known by Him. We want to stand under Abraham's sky with the same twinkle of promise in our eyes, called and connected to the God of the impossible. But first we must unknow what the world has taught us about faith. We must retrace our steps back to the Garden, where the purity of relationship was its own reward.

This homesick world may be in exile, but God is inviting us into a great returning. A return to the purity of His presence, on earth as it is in heaven. He is inviting our prodigal hearts to return to childlike faith. Here, amid our skyscrapers and bottom lines

. . . here, among our crowded news feeds and anxious hearts . . . here, as we mine the meaning within the mysteries of a homesick world, the Father waits for us to return to Him with our whole hearts. God's invitation will always and eventually be to pray our way back, to trust our way back, to risk our way back to childlike hearts. God's prompting will always and eventually be to become more like children, who posture their hearts for curiosity and discovery instead of control and conformity. Impossible seasons have a way of helping us return to the hearts we once had as children. This is the gift in the wound.

Reflection Questions

1. God chose to lay the foundation of His covenantal relationship with Israel on Abraham and Sarah, two unlikely individuals. What does God's choice reveal about His character? What does it reveal about the difference between His Kingdom values and the ways of the world?

2. Hebrews 11:8 tells us that Abraham obeyed God "even though he did not know where he was going." This pivotal moment of radical faith rooted in relational trust changed the course of biblical history. When you are faced with an invitation from God that defies human understanding, what are some personal barriers you may have to trust God with?

3. How do God-given, internal resources differ from external resources in their ability to sustain us through seasons of prolonged perseverance and radical trust?

4. Have you faced an impossible situation in which your own strength or strategies were irrelevant? How did you experience God's presence and provision?

THE UNDOING

Encountering God in Life's Disruptions

My own heart was thrust onto the doorstep of a great undoing at the age of thirteen as my world imploded with one phone call. My mom broke the news to me, and I came face to face with the kind of tragedy that would alter the course of my life. One of my best friends had died by suicide. Facing any level of human loss as a teenager comes with heightened challenges, and my experience was no different. A changing body and the tension of middle school were a recipe for a perfect storm of wild confusion and unyielding grief. Not to mention that when you lose someone you love there is a hollow emptiness and a level of pitch-black sorrow. Dark clouds began to gather over my world. The reality of my own mortality hovered over me for the very first time, an existential crisis a thirteen-year-old brain and body is not developed enough to engage with well. The train of my life had recklessly gone off the tracks, and this was my first experience with capital-*S* Suffering. For the first time I wasn't the empathetic onlooker in my marginalized community. I stood amid the heartbroken and devastated. I did the only thing I knew to do: I dove headlong into what would become a reeducation in childlike faith. I needed to be able to believe in the impossible on the heels of the unthinkable.

As a pastor's daughter, I had heard every version of every major Bible story known to man, and yet my relationship with God had felt somewhat impersonal before this turning point. It was time to find out whether the God who was strong enough to part seas would stoop low enough to come find me. I had heard that every tragedy has the propensity to either draw us closer to God or move us further away from Him, and thus began my intimate journey toward a soul-level friendship with God the Father, the Son, and the Holy Spirit. This would be one of the most unforced decisions of my entire life since pain is the great motivator. I needed consolation from the Comforter Himself. I also began to realize that no one is beyond the reach of suffering and, while heartbreak remains outside God's original design for humanity, I experienced firsthand the way it could draw someone into new heights of intimacy with Him.

My own private crucible of suffering was the very undoing that transformed my distant, conceptual faith into an intimate friendship. As I left the shores of peripheral faith to swim in the deep waters of the biblical narrative, I began to experience a deeper kinship with God. I grieved with Jesus in Gethsemane as He wept in a moonlit garden under the stars He'd once named. I felt His presence when I knelt to pray in my bedroom. I remembered that He, too, was once stretched out on the ground underneath the weight of mystery, and yet He faithfully endured the cross He was given to bear. I began to understand that Jesus is still God with us when we come undone, in every Eden that becomes a Gethsemane. I felt the comfort of the Holy Spirit mark me when sorrow pierced my heart past midnight in moments only under divine observation. And so the day the phone rang with a life-altering loss was also the day that marked the beginning of an undoing that led to a new life of prayer and friendship with my Trinitarian God.

A Childlike Faith

If you've ever visited a playground to watch the sheer delight of children at play you might have observed the reality that a child's joy isn't centered on striving. Childlike joy flows from being present to the moment and simply receiving what is being given: a push on a swing set, a turn down the slide, or a ride on the seesaw. Children play with little regard for control. They believe a loving guardian is nearby, watchful, and trustworthy based on a relational history of safety. Children are humbly dependent and live for the possibility of delight even when they can't quite see it yet. They don't stop taking risks even when the risks they've taken have seemingly betrayed them. They know there's someone loving at the helm who has the grand view of life at heart, so they play on. Jesus invites us all to return to childlikeness:

> "Truly I tell you, unless you change and become like little
> children, you will never enter the kingdom of heaven.
> Therefore, whoever takes the lowly position of this child
> is the greatest in the kingdom of heaven."
> MATTHEW 18:3-4

This is a hard teaching in a grown-up world. So returning to childlike faith usually involves a very personal undoing. In some ways, *all* of life is an undoing; an unknowing of all we thought we knew and an unlearning of all we thought we'd learned—a growing young of sorts. Hebrews 11:1-2 casts vision for what it means to live into this kind of heart posture as it relates to faith:

Faith is confidence in what we hope for and assurance about what we do not see. This is what the ancients were commended for.

Faith is assurance, the same kind of assurance a child has in the authority of a loving caregiver. Childlike faith is rooted in relational exchange with God and a heart willing to answer yes to the core question at the center of every relationship: *Do you trust me?* The answer to this question determines everything. And as is true between a child and a caregiver, nothing less than a relational history of safety can build this level of relational equity over time.

At face value, this sounds beautiful, but dig a little deeper and you'll discover complexity. We live in a world where our emotional availability to trust is marred by our experiences of trust abused, a world where Hebrews 11, childlike trust is often considered blind faith that is neither honorable nor responsible. In our age, so many have replaced a patient posture of listening for the voice of God in prayer with searching for divine direction amid the chaos of a booked and busy pace. Childlike faith swims against this current and flows from the simplicity of a deep reservoir of private intimacy with God.

Hebrews 11 reminds us that the fathers and mothers of our faith flourished not by human strategy or intellectualism but by the force of a faithful friendship with an almighty God. Their faith and the faith of others we will chronicle throughout this book have one important quality in common. Each of these people ultimately lived their life as a sojourner—a sojourner who found their home in a vertically aligned life with God. They understood that this world was shifting sand and set their sights on a home "with foundations, whose architect and builder is God" (Hebrews 11:10).

- Moses' failure led him to the back side of the desert, where his divine calling beckoned to him from a burning bush.
- Joseph spent years in prison under false accusations and traumatic displacement before God ushered him into the fullness of his childhood prophetic dream.
- Mary spent a lifetime living in the tension of Jesus' destined death on the cross before she witnessed the glory of His resurrection and ascension.

What can we learn from this? Typically the winds of God's Spirit come to invite us into the fullness of faith only *after* we've come to the end of ourselves. By this point we no longer want the dream—we just want God Himself. By this point we understand that the cost is too high, but we know there is no option other than surrender. Oftentimes our pain invites us straight into God's presence and becomes a doorway to destiny. If we cooperate with the suffering, we will discover that there's something new He is trying to usher us into. And in this place of unprecedented dependence, we usually stand on the precipice of it all.

But as long as our systems of control are working, we will continue to use them. It is the grace of God, on a soul level, to allow us to experience the failure of these systems. This is when we are best postured to return to childlike faith. Sometimes the ruptures and impossibilities in our stories guide us into a posture of readiness for the long journey of unlearning and relearning, for the transformational return into childlikeness.

And it's worth noting that some of us bear stories in which we experienced this reality well before we were emotionally, physically, mentally, and spiritually prepared to navigate it.

When my own undoing began at the age of thirteen, I had already begun believing the oppressive and paralyzing lie of my own unlikeliness, as a kid from an immigrant mission with over-sized pink glasses. Much like Moses, I was an underdog, plucked out of obscurity. But I felt an inner call to push back on the darkness in the world with the uniquely singular light God has given to all His children, even me. With my smoky, left-of-center alto voice, I prayed there would be a path available to me even if it was the long way. I prayed I would be given the chance to sing us all back home. This grand undoing would mark the beginning of learning how to trade all my plans for the possibility of being surprised by God, a divine invitation Moses was given in a similarly unforced way.

An Underdog Faith

Here in the West, we are mesmerized by stories of underdogs who win. We love Frodo Baggins, a small, unassuming hobbit from the Shire who is chosen for the task of saving the world and succeeds, to the great relief of all mankind. We're inspired by the story of Rudy, who clearly lacks the stature and talent to play Notre Dame football but is chosen against all odds. And let's not forget Remy, from Pixar's beloved 2007 film *Ratatouille*. Remy is the quintessence of unlikely. *Ratatouille* reminds us, "Not everyone can become a great artist, but a great artist can come from anywhere."[1] These amazing stories awaken a sense that we were made for a world where the last really does come first and the meek inherit the earth.

We may love hearing stories *about* the underdog; we just don't want to *be* the underdog because we know we are set in a world system that bends and bows to the powerful, not the unlikely.

I believe the rightness of the upside-down Kingdom of God lives deep down inside us. Long before cultural scripts called the shots, there was just the purity of original love and original relationship. There was a home where everyone had a place and a name that didn't have to be fought for.

As we read in the Bible, Moses' life is a shining example of God's love for the underdog. His first breaths were drawn in the thick air of a treacherous time when all male Hebrew newborns were to be put to death upon Pharaoh's order. As Moses' mother surrendered his infant body along the bank of the Nile to protect him from death, the current of God's sovereign will carried him down the river, away from imminent danger and into Pharaoh's house, a setting that would mark him for destiny. There is no doubt that the circumstances of Moses' birth, upbringing, and life were positioning him for a profound relationship with God, but an undoing would come first. Moses' adventures with God would be one of the greatest stories ever told, lined with glory and personal encounter. The burning bush. The power of God demonstrated through the plagues. The deliverance of God's people through a parted sea, and the miracle of a fire by day and a cloud by night. All these experiences had a cumulative effect on Moses' intimacy with God, which was brought to bear through the sanctum of prayer.

I remember just such a formative moment with God. I was sixteen and had recently discerned a call to ministry. As I took a drive to pray, I was at war with the invitation of God on my life. *You're not beautiful enough. You have no resources. You don't know the right people.* The voice of disqualification was loud. But that day on Farm Road 879, a stirring came to my heart. I had placed my confidence in worldly qualifiers, and these faulty scripts had been given the power to define me to a paralyzing degree. Like Moses, I was caught in the tension of my insecurities and my calling. I needed an encounter with my own burning bush, a fire to light the next part of the path toward my God-given destiny. So I returned to God's Word like the prodigal son returned to his father's house. There I found more evidence that God chooses unlikely people to love, and from that love, those people become light bearers in a world gone dark.

Turning toward the biblical narrative in the face of my insecurities was my Red Sea crossing and the moment I finally accepted God's call. When I crossed onto that long-awaited shore, I reached that side with a conviction to empower others wrestling with their own unlikeliness.

As I moved forward, I did so with conviction and confidence, not in my abilities but in a deep friendship with God and the newfound freedom that came with it.

Going back to the Word to revisit this reality—that God's choice rarely falls in line with human preference—inspired me. I discovered that Moses was an unassuming leader like me. Moses had observed the oppression of his people just as I had observed hatred and discrimination against our minority church community. Moses had a long list of disqualifications. Check. But, like him, I was learning to place my faith in the transformational sanctum of friendship with God. I wouldn't walk into a room with charisma, WOO, or anything the world might deem valuable. But I did know how to walk into *any* space and find God. He was the sun my whole world orbited around.

The years that followed involved a long journey of discovery. There was no clear path of preparation for an unknown girl from a Mexican mission who felt called to care for God's people. But, like Moses, I was the subject of a divinely orchestrated, unsolicited pursuit. I read the Bible every day. I also read Frederick Buechner and Henri Nouwen. I bought leadership conference tickets. I splurged on trainings. I worked forty hours a week to cover my college tuition and walked the stage with a four-year degree I'd completed in four years. I listened to hundreds of audiobooks. I spent decades serving as a leader in the local church. And then one day, something significant clicked.

Like Moses, I found that the flame of the fullness of my call had been lit for me as I set out for my third nationwide tour as a singer-songwriter, worship leader, and speaker. I left for the road with the same sincere intent as every tour before, but night after night I observed a shift in the audience. After the concert, instead of awkward autograph requests, people lined up for prayer and hands-on ministry. *Feed my sheep* had been a whisper to my soul for what had felt like a lifetime, but now this invitation was fully embodied. I looked into real faces. I heard real stories. I prayed real prayers. I witnessed real tears. The activity of God in new stories and faces became my cloud by day and fire by night. But, much like for the Israelites, arriving at this moment represented a journey. A journey of patience Moses knew very well—and a transformational path that had begun with an undoing.

Moses' Undoing

I'll lead with the bad news: In this post-Eden world, we are all born into the inevitable reality of longing and the likelihood of a great disruption. The good news? This disruption has the potential to usher us through the doorway of a deep, abiding friendship with God, should we choose to take the narrow road that leads to life in Him. I call this process *the undoing*. This is a space in our journey where we become untethered from

- our systems of control,
- the answers we once depended upon, and
- the outcomes we once pursued.

Within the undoing, the paths in our lives that once felt like maximum-speed highways become dead ends. Instead of hurtling along at a frantic pace, we find ourselves parked at a fork in the road, wondering where to go next. Our willingness to engage with God at the intersection of this undoing determines whether we will die on the hill of our former selves or fall forward into divinely led transformation. The onset of the undoing is usually only made possible by a great disruption because this is *the* revelatory experience that exposes former solutions as ineffective and unsatisfying. There is no doubt that the circumstances of Moses' birth and upbringing were one great disruption that would position him for the fullness of a call to deliver God's people. He would rescue the sheep who had come undone without a shepherd, but his own undoing would come first.

> It came to pass in those days, when Moses was grown, that he went out to his brethren and looked at their burdens. And he saw an Egyptian beating a Hebrew, one of his brethren. So he looked this way and that way, and when he saw no one, he killed the Egyptian and hid him in the sand. And when he went out the second day, behold, two Hebrew men were fighting, and he said to the one who did the wrong, "Why are you striking your companion?"
>
> Then he said, "Who made you a prince and a judge over us? Do you intend to kill me as you killed the Egyptian?"
>
> So Moses feared and said, "Surely this thing is known!" When Pharaoh heard of this matter, he sought to kill Moses. But Moses fled from the face of Pharaoh and dwelt in the land of Midian; and he sat down by a well.
>
> EXODUS 2:11-15, NKJV

Injustice. Anger. Hurt. Harm. Fear. Unresolved pain bubbling underneath the surface of our lives eventually reveals itself. The great disruption in Moses' interior life became visible to the world around him in the form of a significant rupture. At the sight of his people being oppressed, Moses killed a man . . . and then fled for his life. As a result, he left

- his systems of control,
- the answers he had once depended upon, and
- the outcomes he had once pursued.

Author Ruth Haley Barton describes this season of Moses' life this way:

> The first leg of Moses' journey as a leader, then, was not to lead anyone else anywhere; it was to allow himself to be led into freedom from his own bondage. Before he could lead others into freedom, he needed to experience freedom himself. In solitude he was able to let go of the coping mechanisms that had served him well in the past but were completely inappropriate for the leader he was becoming.[2]

Moses' exile would change the trajectory of his life. His undoing would hold the same potential every undoing we experience holds: the potential to usher us beyond a peripheral understanding of God as a concept and into a face-to-face encounter with God as a person, a process that prepares us to live into the fullness of our God-given design.

Encounter

If we live long enough, we will become well acquainted with disruptions and undoings, but if our hearts are aimed upward, we will discover unforced gifts carried on the current of those winds. When we study the biblical narrative, we see that the wilderness can be a formative experience where friendship with God is forged in the fires of dependence. We see wilderness silence as a teacher who helps us understand how to be alone but not lonely. In the silence of the desert, all that has distracted us from facing our inner life with God has been removed. It is the place where the silence can be filled with what Dallas Willard refers to as a "conversational relationship" with God.[3]

Prayer is that holy and honest space where God ceases to be a concept held only in our minds and instead becomes a person we talk to and engage with. There's a critical difference between faith in a concept and faith in a person. The difference is relational exchange. In the sanctum of prayer, God invites us to shed the weight of performance and to simply enter just as we are.

I've always found it incredibly intriguing that in the aftermath of Moses' own undoing he found himself on the back side of the desert in the long descent of humility. He had sojourned from the royal house of Pharaoh to the lowly position of tending sheep. Humility is the biblical prerequisite for greatness, and as Moses was surrounded by the bleating of sheep, he found himself in the epicenter of Meekness 101. With the sting of failure fresh upon his heart, he survived his own undoing. In God's mercy, the end is the beginning.

Who is this who speaks out of the burning bush? God's grand introduction as the Great I Am included signs and wonders.

> When the LORD saw that he had gone over to look, God
> called to him from within the bush, "Moses! Moses!"
> And Moses said, "Here I am."
>
> EXODUS 3:4

Disruption and undoing do not have to be in vain. They are frequently mile markers on the journey to radical encounter. Encounter is a fork in the road—the place where a conceptual brush with God is exchanged for a visceral experience with Him as a person. In the face of encounter, there is only one thing to do: respond. To be clear: One can choose to move on from the encounter without entering a relationship. Moses chose the other option. Moses took his shoes off because he was in the presence of a personal, almighty God. God radiates holiness. He is other, and He was about to change the trajectory of Moses' life. This is what encounters do. This is how we know whether we're immersed in faith in a concept or faith in a person. The difference is the moments that mark us through relationship. The difference is transformation. While the details of a transformation are unique to the individual, the path to it tends to follow this process:

Disruption $\longrightarrow$ Undoing $\longrightarrow$ Encounter $\longrightarrow$ Friendship $\longrightarrow$ Transformation

In Moses' case, God introduced Himself and then invited Moses into the sanctum of friendship where he would be fully formed to live into the completeness of his God-given design for God's glory, Moses' own good, and the deliverance of God's people. Every conversation with God would become a conduit for his own spiritual formation.

Prayer

God's heartbeat for humanity has always been relationship. As such, prayer is the pathway for proximity to God, an act of vulnerability rooted in trust.

In Richard Foster's book *Celebration of Discipline: The Path to Spiritual Growth,* he speaks to the importance of prayer and the tension some feel around this practice:

> Human beings seem to have a perpetual tendency to have
> somebody else talk to God for them. . . . The history of
> religion is the story of an almost desperate scramble to
> have a king, a mediator, a priest, a pastor, a go-between.
> In this way we do not need to go to God ourselves. Such
> an approach saves us from the need to change, for to be
> in the presence of God is to change.[4]

Moses modeled what it means to enter the purity of knowing and being known since his life with God was not transactional but relational. In God's heart, Moses' primary name and role would not be *deliverer* but *friend.*

All friendships are built in the same way: an ocean of time together fed by the streams of honesty, vulnerability, and commitment. One of the first lessons God would teach Moses is that being on mission for Him does not replace being in communion with Him. Moses would not just become a person of influence *for* God; he would develop an intimate relationship *with* God through a lifelong journey of prayerful dependence. Why is this conversation important in our present age? We are a prayerless people, and our prayerlessness produces a conceptual approach to God in which we are prone to tend to the cultural requirements of faith but fail to relate to God privately as a friend. This can happen to both the spiritually immature and the seemingly spiritually mature. No one is exempt from succumbing to a peripheral view of God, laypersons and leaders alike.

For example, the average person may live this out practically by subscribing to a weekly rhythm of church attendance with a desire to earn religious good standing without spending a quantity of quality time with God. Then there are those who are spiritually mature but lack the discernment to value friendship with God over their missional work in His name. In the words of Pete Scazzero, their doing for God exceeds their being with Him.[5]

Here in the West, our prayerlessness has a name: distraction. And our lack of prayerful proximity to God results in a lack of intimacy. We can know a lot about a person intellectually but not prioritize communication with that person, and our experience with them will never translate into heart connection. Prayer is the circulatory system for our relational blood flow with God. It keeps our intimacy with Him healthy and alive. When we neglect to prioritize this practice as a culture, there are far-reaching implications.

How is this displayed? When our platforms are filled with people who meet the exterior, culturally esteemed qualifications but do not have a robust interior life with God (the kind that produces the fruit of the Spirit), our prayerlessness has poisoned the well of our discernment. We see this when public perception is more highly regarded than private devotion and when entire ministries are wagered on talent and charisma at the expense of integrity before God and personal holiness.

Man looks at the outside; God looks at the heart (1 Samuel 16:7). Moses replied to God's invitation to deliver His people with a host of disqualifications, including his lack of eloquence and slowness of speech. Yet Moses was not qualified by his capabilities but through his willingness to meet with God consistently, to embark on an intimate journey of relational dependence:

Moses said to the LORD, "Pardon your servant, Lord. I have never been eloquent, neither in the past nor since

41

you have spoken to your servant. I am slow of speech and tongue."

The LORD said to him, "Who gave human beings their mouths? Who makes them deaf or mute? Who gives them sight or makes them blind? Is it not I, the LORD? Now go; I will help you speak and will teach you what to say."

EXODUS 4:10-12

Dependence

Dependence is an essential transitional component that leads us away from conceptual religion and into relational intimacy. It is a gift no one would ask for, but it's a nonnegotiable component to a thriving friendship with God. Moses commits murder and then flees to the back side of the desert with no plan, so he was uniquely positioned for relational dependence. God often chooses unlikely people because He knows they are beautifully primed to reject autonomy. In our humanity, we are drawn to God more often by necessity than desire. Moses needed the personal presence of God to meet him at the intersection of his insufficiency and his calling, and God was faithful to draw him near. Dependence is still God's invitation to His people today. To accept it, we must begin untethering ourselves from the cultural status quo of formulaic thinking.

Concepts can be mastered. Relationships are complex.

Concepts can live in a space where faith is entirely cerebral, where our hearts and humanity are withheld. Relationships are not equations to be solved. They are developmental journeys where joy and disappointment and depth cannot be controlled but must be experienced.

Concepts have the potential to become nothing more than a

means to a desired end that is achieved—not received—through intellectual mastery. Relational dependence is nourished by vulnerability and real-time, real-life exchanges in prayer.

The invitation of a relationship-first God is so much deeper than conceptual understanding, and Moses' dependence helped him grasp this intimately. Like Moses I might've said, *Pardon your servant, Lord. Please send someone else* a hundred times over the years. For decades I sat at the piano in private worship and wept at God's audacity at asking a Latina woman, a double minority in the church, to feed His sheep. *How am I to do this?* Like Moses I was at war with God for choosing me. But over time God has shown me that in His Kingdom there are no anomalies; there are only possibilities.

The great disruptions and undoings in our lives have the potential to usher us into encounters with God that revive our prayers, transform our relationships with Him, and influence our destinies. We see evidence of this in the contrast between Moses' burning bush encounter and the eventual full acceptance of his call to lead God's people through what became a pivotal turning point in Israel's history. When Moses prayed, "Show me your glory" (Exodus 33:18), he had untethered himself from human outcomes and instead fully longed to know and see God as a person.

> As Moses went into the tent, the pillar of cloud would come down and stay at the entrance, while the LORD spoke with Moses. Whenever the people saw the pillar of cloud standing at the entrance to the tent, they all stood and worshiped, each at the entrance to their tent. The LORD would speak to Moses face to face, as one speaks to a friend.
>
> EXODUS 33:9-11

Moses' great disruption, his very personal undoing, and his encounter with the Lord became what we all long for: an intimate, soul-level friendship with God. The rupture of his origin story, the Egyptian plagues, the Red Sea crossing, meeting God on Mount Sinai . . . these moments and a multitude of private ones in between resulted in a sacred journey of Moses befriending God while becoming equipped to steward a calling that involved the highest highs and the lowest lows.

From the heights of miraculous mountaintop moments to the depths of frustration and failure, Moses learned how to shepherd others from the Great Shepherd Himself. God's presence grounded him to lead a people who were rebellious, forgetful, and often bent on betrayal. And Moses coexisted with those lived realities by calling upon a greater reality: God Himself, who loves us through our cynicism and distrust and holds out His hand in a million ways to accompany us back home. Moses' model for love was One who is love. This is how he endured, and this is how we endure.

The invitation God gave to Moses is the same one He extends to us today: to grow beyond the size of our fears and into the power of a life formed by companionship with God. To allow our longing for God's glory and our desire for intimacy with Him to be the Promised Land we yearn for, the experience of a real-time, living-and-breathing relationship with God as a person and not a principle. To be certain of this: There is still smoke on the mountain, a God working all things for our good, who has already prepared a place of rest, instruction, and strength in the permanent home of prayer and friendship.

Reflection Questions

1. Have you ever experienced a great undoing that eventually led to transformation? How did God meet you through this experience?

2. Where do you find yourself in the journey of transformation as you consider this visual of the process?

    Disruption → Undoing → Encounter → Friendship → Transformation

3. Why is prayer so important in cultivating a friendship with God?

4. What is the defining quality that made Moses a faithful leader of God's people?

REDEEMING THE STORY

Translating the Reality of Suffering

The Mexican mission my parents have pastored for forty years is on Avenue A and is located, to this day, in an area of town the locals call Little Mexico. On any given Sunday afternoon, you may hear the paletero ringing his bell outside to draw attention to his paleta cart. A lime or banana paleta, the Mexican version of a frozen-fruit popsicle, is the best way to take the edge off the Texas heat.

Before paletas became all the rage in hipster communities across America, the original palatero, Juan Pablo, was in our neighborhood. He took care of our congregation, and we took care of him. He came fully stocked, and we bought him out. This wasn't simply supply and demand; this was our value of solidarity in suffering on full display. When one person had a problem or need in our community, it was not just their problem, it was our problem. Ambivalence and self-sufficiency were not options. Suffering was a communal experience, and we always had a collective response. We knew how to have each other's backs, and when we said we were going to do something, follow-through was guaranteed. Often the mental, emotional, spiritual, physical, and relational health of our congregation hung in the balance.

In many circles in Hispanic culture, it's not uncommon for lines between a church service and a family gathering to be blurred, because in a culture of family, they often feel like the same thing. On Sundays in our community, discipleship classes began at 8:30 a.m., church service started at 11:00 a.m., and we typically ended around 2:00 p.m. If relationships flourish around a quantity of quality time, our reservoir of quality time would never be low. In our culture, this translated into full-circle, healthy interdependence. The person who prayed with you at the altar at the end of service might also be the person who served you fajitas after the "amen" or who brought groceries to your doorstep if your family was in need. The person who helped you park that morning might also be the person who dug a hole in the backyard to cook a goat in for a community-wide meal or who met you on the side of the road if you had car trouble.

You get the picture: We were all connected. There were no such things as distant, transactional relationships in our community. We didn't always write checks for goods or services. We were not fluent in the language of transactionalism. If someone in the community had the necessary gifting or the resources, we called on them (and felt safe enough to do so). Generosity was a form of relational currency. We lived with an "it takes a village" mindset. The result was nearness—close relationships in proximity. Consistency. Unity. Loyalty. Interdependence. We did not clock in and clock out of each other's lives. The church was not a building; *we* were the church. As I look back in the rearview mirror, I'm certain the glue that held these core values together was the suffering among us. Yes, suffering. The needs existing among us united us because they were the air we all breathed.

We all lived within earshot of a constant drip of trouble. In the absence of the cultural currencies of money and power, we had the Kingdom currencies of love and kindness. In the absence of our ability to take on the attributes the world esteemed, we sought to embody the attributes of God. We learned to see the suffering of the world and one another through the perspective of a God who is compassionate, slow to anger, and abounding in love (Psalm 103:8). We learned how to comfort from a God who extended comfort as a mother comforts a child. We learned how to advocate from a God whose justice and power parted seas and shut the mouths of lions. We didn't have high-dollar conferences with world-renowned speakers and fancy greenrooms. We had God Himself, and we learned from Him. We knew He was for us. We felt His presence and were changed. We were baptized in the formational fires of suffering, and we were purified by it on a soul level.

I often define *suffering* as any condition in which we feel powerless and that causes uninvited distress. It is both singular and collective. It is the invisible common denominator of all ailments of mind, body, and heart, the thick air we all breathe in a post-Eden world. It is the central experience encompassing all human heartbreak.

There is no fire escape we can take to avoid its flames. No formula, fix, or miracle on this side of heaven can nullify the reality of its reach. We cannot avoid suffering, but we can be formed by it. As fourth-century theologian Saint Augustine is often credited with saying, "God had one son on earth without sin, but never one without suffering."

Befriending God in Suffering

I have always believed Joseph's story to be a signal fire for those of us who have experienced the long-term effects of uninvited trouble. Those of us for whom the fires of pain don't die down with a petition or two (or one hundred). His story is for those of us who know what it's like to call the desert—a wilderness of sustained heat with little reprieve—home.

As difficult as it is, the person who learns how to engage with God amid mystery and suffering will have a fuller and more complete grasp on what it means to truly befriend Him. The byproduct of suffering with God is an intimacy with Him that will endure through the seasons. But first we must admit that there are questions and situations in our lives that cannot be explained. First we have to resist the temptation to fill in the blank with inadequate answers when a question mark best honors the moment we find ourselves in. When we are left with no language and our formulas and fixes have failed us, we are forced to go beyond conceptual faith and into the depths of intimate dialogue with a relationship-first God who has a bird's-eye view over all life.

In the ground of our lives, hardship is often the soil in which we learn to invite God to have full access for deeper work: a deeper faith, a deeper hope, and a deeper love. Sometimes, like He did with Joseph, God will allow us to weather the winds of suffering so He can strengthen our roots and cultivate the gardens of our devotion to Him.

When we are able to acknowledge that there is only one God who sends the sun and the rain, we can confess our powerlessness and surrender the fields of our lives into His care. We can invite Him in to nourish our roots to grow where they have been planted—even though we might have chosen a different field. We can partner with God to produce beauty and bounty in places we thought were beyond hope and harvest and yield to His sovereign love, a love that is continuously engaged in the work of redeeming the seemingly irredeemable.

Joseph, son of Jacob, illustrates this process beautifully since he has one of the most extensive stories of suffering in the biblical narrative. He was his father's favorite, born to him in old age. Jacob was not discreet about his favor toward Joseph, and he presented him with a lavish coat of many colors. Not only was Joseph the recipient of Jacob's favor, but he also had the gift of prophecy, and he shared his dreams and interpretations with others. Joseph's siblings seethed with envy at this radical favoritism and spiritual gifting, giving us a glimpse into the reality that envy is often the relational curse that accompanies favor. In Joseph's story, envy led to hatred, and hatred led to displacement when he was ultimately sold into slavery by his brothers. This propelled Joseph on a thirteen-year journey of formation through the fires of suffering.

When Joseph was thrust into the despair of slavery, his inner life expanded as he learned how to relate to God outside the blessing of favor and within the lingering ache of all that could not be explained or understood. Joseph found himself in the wake of

- family betrayal,
- total abandonment, and
- broken dreams.

On the surface it appeared as if Joseph's life was over. Suffering has a way of convincing us of its finality. On the heels of two prophetic dreams, Joseph suffered the death of the life he knew and was in a strange land in the hands of strangers. But he was not without his God.

There is an important refrain in Joseph's story: *The Lord was with him.*

The LORD was with Joseph, and he was a successful man; and he was in the house of his master the Egyptian. And his master saw that *the LORD was with him* and that the LORD made all he did to prosper in his hand. So Joseph found favor in his sight, and served him. Then he made him overseer of his house, and all that he had he put under his authority. So it was, from the time that he had made him overseer of his house and all that he had, that the LORD blessed the Egyptian's house for Joseph's sake; and the blessing of the LORD was on all that he had in the house and in the field. Thus he left all that he had in Joseph's hand, and he did not know what he had except for the bread which he ate.

GENESIS 39:2-6, NKJV (EMPHASIS ADDED)

In these opening passages of his story, we see that in spite of Joseph's displacement, God's favor and presence followed him even when, by all appearances, the ruptures in Joseph's life seemed beyond repair. This is a very important distinction for us to grasp. In the West, our culture assumes that God's favor is most likely removed from a person who experiences the removal of people's favor. But this assumption is not in sync with what we learn from the biblical narrative. The stories of the fathers and mothers of our faith reveal that suffering and trouble are both confirmations of and close companions to those who befriend God intimately here in a post-Eden world. In Genesis we see that God's loving relational gaze is set on Joseph as a victim of injustice. God's smile is not contingent on faulty man-made power structures and the fallibility of free will. He works in mysterious ways, and this Scripture passage reveals that God shows favor to those who remain in Him, regardless of whether human power structures do so.

When we look at Joseph's suffering through the lens of God's sovereignty, faithfulness, and justice, we will find that God's character established and strengthened essential root systems of faith, hope, and love in Joseph's life.

God's Sovereignty

In the wake of betrayal and displacement at the hands of his jealous brothers, Joseph was strategically placed in Pharaoh's house. God's sovereignty can see in places we cannot, and His providential hand can be trusted. Although Joseph did not understand in real time, he was being strategically positioned for three important things: (1) favor (despite unfavorable circumstances), (2) godly character, and (3) relationships that would be essential to the salvation of God's people.

In the wake of betrayal, God shepherded Joseph's heart and nourished the root system of his faith, proving that He could be trusted to sovereignly work Joseph's displacement out for his good and others'.

God's Faithfulness

When Joseph was imprisoned after being falsely accused by Potiphar's wife, God proved once again that He is close to the brokenhearted and crushed in spirit (Psalm 34:18). God's favor and presence followed Joseph even as he entered the depths of trauma. Joseph's heart was centered in God's righteousness amid circumstantial rises and falls, and thus God granted him favor even in prison. Joseph's radical loyalty to God in private positioned him for public favor later. The light of God's faithfulness penetrated every layer of Joseph's suffering, nourishing the seed of his hope and helping him realize that no season of suffering is final.

God's Justice

In one moment, Joseph moved from a prison to a palace. God can do in an instant what it would take us decades to try to accomplish in our own strength. This is an important teaching in a "do more, try harder" culture. Scripture is clear: When God's timeline for redemption is activated, no man can thwart His plan. And yet there are many dimensions to redemption. While Joseph's circumstantial suffering had been lifted, there was still a dark, thick cloud of anguish hovering over his heart. As he was released from his unjust prison sentence, he was still bound by an invisible prison—his past.

Joseph had been through the process with God for over a decade. He now had the blessing of a family and had been elevated into a position of influence after years of displacement, betrayal, and trauma. And if it had all ended here, it would be one incredible success story. But God wants more for us than visible success. He desires soul-level wholeness and healing for each one of His children. He not only has the power to restore what was lost; He has the power to heal what was broken. God wanted more for Joseph than mere titles, influence, achievement, and earthly security: He wanted to repair his broken heart.

In keeping with God's loving character, He orchestrated a reunion with the very same brothers who had thrust Joseph into suffering. This reunion culminated in complete relational reconciliation, the redemption of Joseph's trauma, and the salvation of God's people. But this scene in Scripture reveals one important relational quality not to be missed. God desired to lovingly relate to Joseph beyond usefulness, and the same is true for you and me. In a transactional world, so many of us settle for being useful to God when what we really want is to be wholly loved and made whole by Him. Here we observe that God does not see Joseph as a role. He sees him as a beating heart, a heart in desperate need of care. God is not transactional; He is relational, and this is proven throughout the biblical narrative.

Relationship Is the Goal

You are not a role to God. You are a beating heart. Those who have a transactional view of God place the template of a transactional culture onto a God who doesn't fit the mold. His love will not be boxed in by titles and bottom lines . . . algorithms and likes . . . ones and zeros. He will turn every one of those tables over in our hearts until we understand that His love is not for sale. You and I cannot perform for the open door of our belongingness in Him. He longs to love us just because He is love. Joseph's destiny was not simply to be useful in the Kingdom of God. His destiny, like ours, was to be led by the hand into a loving relationship with God as a friend and to allow this intimacy to shepherd him through forgiveness and into radical trust, a trust that would result in what we all long for: a special relationship with God. A relationship that would bear the fruit of full surrender to a process with God, through suffering, that produced a heart that allowed him to stand in front of his abusers and extend love, reconciliation, and grace.

What was true for Joseph all those centuries ago is also true for us today. Trouble is an invitation to move closer to God, not further away. The result, over a lifetime of process, is not aimed at human utopia, earthly security, worldly advancement, or any other gain. God wants so much more for us than the American Dream. The goal for Joseph's endurance through suffering is the same as for you and me: to bear the fruit of righteousness and to take our place in God's Kingdom as people of character capable of displaying His radiant light through faith, hope, and love as the world grows dim and dark.

As Joseph found himself in the darkness of suffering, a sacred formational fire was being stoked within through each traumatic event. He discovered that it was not his own strength, nor the force of his own resilience, that guided him through the long shadows of mystery. God was stoking the smoldering wick of redemption, even in the darkness. Joseph's suffering would not be for its own sake but would reveal the beauty and steadfastness of God's attributes and His power to form Joseph into the fullness of all he was created for through the most difficult of circumstances.

Equations and formulas are powerless against the force of life's great mysteries. A concept does nothing to deliver us in the middle of a dark night of the soul. A person does. *God* does. It is His loyal love and faithfulness that can supernaturally intervene in our natural circumstances to supernatural ends.

> You intended to harm me, but God intended it for good
> to accomplish what is now being done, the saving of
> many lives.
> GENESIS 50:20

Joseph learned to lean into the presence of God amid suffering. This is one of the keys of deeper discipleship.

I was six years old when God called us to leave Godley, Texas, and move to the town of Ennis. Everything about this season was new; we left a population-300 town for a population-13,000 community. I can feel the butterflies in my stomach now—a low-humming anticipation meets a fear-of-the-unknown kind of feeling. I remember the first time I walked into the parsonage they offered to us as part of our compensation for coming to pastor a Mexican American mission that had been floundering. It was a modest, twelve-hundred-ish-square-foot home. The carpet looked original; the linoleum floors did as well. Each gave 1960s vibes. The footprint was tiny, but I was, too, and from my vantage point as a second grader, a small home felt like a warm hug hemming me into safety.

As time passed, our tiny home began to feel tinier. The teenage years ushered in Super Bowl youth parties, Christmas gatherings, and the like. We were bursting at the seams. We did the best we could, but as my brother and I left for college, the house never entered a period of dormancy. If those walls could speak, they would tell you story after story of marriages mended, immigrant families encountering hope, the suicidal kept safe, the battered woman who found refuge. Our home, like our church, was a conduit for the gospel. Our home was a hospital for the sick, and it was not ours; it belonged to everyone. It was a communal haven, and we saw it as such. But as my parents aged, the tiny ranch home on a hill became a crucible when one outpatient surgery resulted in an accident that rendered my dad unable to walk ever again. In the blink of an eye, our whole world changed.

Mom became a full-time caretaker for him, and the tiny parsonage we'd always seemed to manage our way around became unfit for our family overnight. The living room turned into a hospital room, complete with a hospital bed and one chair. The kitchen and hallway were overflowing with medical supplies and devices. Our hearts sank under the weight of the finality of it all.

When you're called to minister to a marginalized community, a group of individuals who work difficult blue-collar jobs to make ends meet and raise funds for most auxiliary needs in the church, there isn't a stash of cash somewhere to give the pastor a raise or to help him modify his home. The people brought food to our doorstep. They safely transported Dad back and forth to the hospital and to doctors' visits. They did this for almost seven years. *We* carried the emotional weight of this for almost seven years until God wrote a beautiful plot twist into the story.

One day, a builder darkened the doorstep of our tiny parsonage and presented my dad with the seed of a God dream. He came to say he wanted to build our family a new home, a home that would be handicap accessible and meet the needs present due to my dad's disabilities. Dad was cautiously optimistic and began to work with him to brainstorm about how this would come to pass. The inevitable hurdle was the same hurdle that had been present since day one in Godley, Texas: In a community absent of wealth, resources are more than an arm's length away. But God had set a supernatural dream in motion, and it would not be thwarted by a lack of strategy, funds, or connections.

The church I grew up in was known for many things: loud music, long services, big meals, and what we call la coperacha (translation: the cooperative community effort). Quinceañeras, weddings, funerals . . . events were built around the foundational belief that the entire community would step in together to provide what an individual or individual family alone could not financially provide themselves.

And an entire community of Hispanic pastors and their wives would willingly step into the organization of this project to make sure a seemingly impossible dream home more suitable for my dad's disability would be made possible. A special building-fund account was set up where members of our Mexican mission, along with pastors and leaders of the greater Dallas–Fort Worth community, could make contributions on behalf of my parents. Month by month the account increased, and eventually it grew to fit the size of the dream an entire community rallied to bring to fruition. Much like with the events in Godley, God was redeeming the story of His people through His people. Contractors began to donate concrete, shingles, lumber, and labor. One woman donated $35,000 to provide the exterior brick and labor. The generosity was staggering. People from every corner and facet of the Hispanic community heard of this God dream and came from far and wide to give of their time, talents, and treasures to a family who had laid their lives on the altar of the gospel. And they didn't just offer to do the minimum. Their hearts were set on honor, and when our hearts are set on honor, we will go above and beyond what is expected.

I will never forget the day my family and I drove up to a gorgeous forty-five-hundred-square-foot home on a 1.2-acre lot in a beautiful subdivision. I wept tears of relief and disbelief. I stood in awe as I walked in to see my mom and dad settling into their brand-new home after years of sowing their lives into the gospel. Dad was now able to move about freely in his wheelchair through wider hallways and doorways and rooms. His freedom and dignity had been restored. My mother, who had labored intensively to care for him, given the worst of circumstances, could now do so with greater sustainability.

My parents had laid their lives down in an obscure church in an obscure town. They had answered thousands of unpaid telephone calls from immigrants desperate for help. They had clothed and fed the hungry. They had visited the sick in hundreds of hospital visits. They had fasted, prayed, and sought the face of God faithfully in private and in public for forty-seven years. They had not built their own brand, hoping to draw the approval of man. They lived for the approval of God and carried the aroma of Christ wherever they were led. They were not like "so many [others, who] peddle the word of God for profit. On the contrary, in Christ [they spoke] before God with sincerity, as those sent from God" (2 Corinthians 2:17).

They had been led by the hand to the humblest of circumstances, shepherded a community the world might overlook, but in God's grand vision for my parents' life, each act of love in Jesus' name was a seed. Over forty-seven years, countless seeds had been scattered in thousands of lives. As God would have it, the fields were now ripe for harvest. My parents had sown their lives in nothing less than the gospel. And having rejected the world's view of success and embraced the meek, they would be taken care of in supernatural, miraculous ways. God made certain of that.

In a family-oriented culture, the relationship-building attributes of a relationship-first God—His compassion, mercy, and love—are ones the community strives hardest to emulate. Our people had decided not to abandon the family who had spiritually, physically, emotionally, and relationally nourished them for forty-seven years. In Spanish we have this saying: "Él que quiere puede"—"He who wants to *can*." Our people wanted to see God redeem our story as a family, and they banded together with their full yes to God to see it come to pass.

In our struggle with my father's disability and the crisis in our home, we learned this best: Our communion with God amid suffering imparts the most sustaining power. Before God's redemptive heart was demonstrated through an entire network of pastors, leaders, and congregants who miraculously united to bless our family with a new home, we had spent seven years allowing the storm to spiritually form us. In the belly of the beast, we knew our trouble was under divine observation long before there was a collective response to it. We had been carried beyond human certainty and delivered into the deep end of the ocean of faith, where we saw the color of the water change. The storm had drawn us out into the wildness of the wonder of mystery. There we caught the current of God's presence into new horizons, where the waters of our faith were crystalline and open-ended. *What would God do? Where would He lead? How would He provide?* We forfeited our right to know as we yielded to the Captain of the storm. We knew our suffering was an invitation to the wonder of the waves, where a confluence of intimacy and possibility would make us new. We were baptized in surrender long before we were surprised by the flow of God's supernatural intervention through our community, a community who publicly embodied the loving attributes of God we had been experiencing privately in the secret place with Him.

I don't know where you find yourself in this season of life. Maybe you are on the shores of predictability and safety, or perhaps you have been tossed out into the wildness of an unsettled sea. Here's what I want you to hear: There is an invitation in the suffering. There is an invitation in the mystery. Because in the absence of answers and in the absence of understanding, God offers us what we truly need: more of Him.

In this very moment, your heart is under divine observation. *You are not alone.* I invite you to let these words wash over you and to remember that no season is final where God's redemptive heart and hand are present. He is in the work of redeeming the story, from every day to eternity.

[The LORD said,] "When you pass through the waters,
    I will be with you;
and when you pass through the rivers,
    they will not sweep over you.

When you walk through the fire,
    you will not be burned;
    the flames will not set you ablaze."
ISAIAH 43:2

Reflection Questions

1. What does Joseph's life teach us about God's relational presence in our suffering?

2. God is not transactional; He is relational. What tables need to be turned over in your heart for you to receive the purity of His love for you . . . simply because *He* is love?

3. How can we display God's value for the fact that everyone we meet is not a role but a beating heart?

4. Redemption is multidimensional and goes far beyond outward success and into inner wholeness. Which invisible areas in your life still need to experience God's redemptive touch?

4

HEART OPEN, WALLS DOWN

Learning God's Honest Language

I've always had a soft spot for David. Young David built his relationship with God while herding sheep. I built mine in the quiet Texas plains. Both origin stories involved green pastures, singing, and the Presence. His vulnerability, creativity, and unsanitized prayers have always felt like a mirror to my soul. David is an artist's artist, and his temperament is a wild, crashing wave in an ocean of personalities in the biblical narrative. Nevertheless, it's clear that God didn't just tolerate David—He liked David and He loved him. As someone with an artist's temperament, I've always found this deeply comforting.

We read in 1 Samuel 16:7: "The LORD does not look at the things people look at. People look at the outward appearance, but the LORD looks at the heart."

This passage has always felt like perfect language to describe God's priority for the invisible condition of man's heart, and it serves as a fitting prologue to David's story. David was the last in line of Jesse's sons, a shepherd boy who would one day serve as the third king of Israel. His numerous giftings and callings included musician (harpist), songwriter, warrior, and distinguished leader of God's people. David is most notable for penning many of the Psalms, which give us insight into the immense joys and sorrows present in a foundational friendship with God here in this post-Eden world. His psalms reveal a faith that would flourish in the interior landscape of David's heart and would teach generations to come of the importance of an emotionally honest life with God. And while David's human flaws and failings are well documented through Scripture, we see his intimate relational closeness with God preserved through repentance and humility. This level of intimate friendship rooted in vulnerability stands in contrast to a world that has always praised performance, exterior appearances, and shallow superficiality over the depth of unsanitized truth.

David's earliest beginnings were set against the backdrop of silence and solitude with God. I've never met a contemplative-artist type who doesn't spend oceans of time protecting their aloneness. Artists need space. We need open fields of green, quiet meadows, and solitude under the stars. We need space to reflect, listen, imagine, and dream. We need distance from the world to contemplate the questions no one seems to be asking out loud. It is my belief that every good thing that lies dormant in an artist can be activated with enough silence and solitude to encourage it to the surface. Before I acquired any book knowledge about this subject, this was the natural, unforced inner ebb and flow of my life. I spent the lion's share of my time alone. Dreaming. Thinking. Observing. Discerning.

Like David, this is how my relational intimacy with God began. There in the open Texas plains, I spoke to Him. As the wind moved across the open fields of wheat and the sun set in unnamed shades of orange, I had honest conversations with God. Removed from the distractions of the world in rural Texas, I had ample space to cultivate a heart fully present to God and to my own emotions and the margin to engage with Him in the quiet. Over time these conversations grew into the depths of familiar friendship. God was not a distant concept. He was my person.

I guess it's no surprise I began to lovingly refer to Him as the Original Artist from a young age. He was the first to make something beautiful out of absolutely nothing, which is what artists do. He painted the first colors onto the canvas of creation. He spoke the first sounds. He *is* the Original Artist, and all creation is His song. *We* are His song. For as long as I can remember, God's creativity has been one of the primary love languages in our relationship. It's almost as if from one artist to another, God knew the way to my heart.

David understood how God speaks through the wonder of the world He made. He understood that wonder is relational at its core. He wrote about this in Psalm 19:1-4:

> The heavens declare the glory of God;
> > the skies proclaim the work of his hands.
> Day after day they pour forth speech;
> > night after night they reveal knowledge.
> They have no speech, they use no words;
> > no sound is heard from them.
> Yet their voice goes out into all the earth.

For David, like for me, creation was, in essence, a conduit for connection with God and a living illustration of His love. Creation was a place where solitude and silence under a blue sky could become a prompt for sincere worship and vulnerable prayers. David knew what I somehow knew inherently growing up: Relationships are cultivated over a quantity of quality time and through honest communication.

In my life, these two truths met against the backdrop of God's creation—a place where, as Romans 1:20 describes, God's invisible qualities were made visible. This was a space where every sunrise and sunset was like a whisper to my soul, saying, *You can be sure of Me.* There was only one thing to do in the face of the very personal awe of these moments: respond. Emotional honesty with God always drew me to response. Sometimes I responded through prayer. Sometimes I responded through worshipful song. Sometimes I responded through tears, but I always responded.

This was the weekly, daily, hourly rhythm of my first steps under the shadow of His wings, and this is a language David knew well. The quantity of quality time David spent communing with God alone was the birthplace of the Psalms and the inception of a level of intimate trust that would be required for him to eventually enter the fullness of God's invitation over his life. There is so much to be learned from David's beginnings. His starting line is a helpful marker for our own, and Psalm 139:1-18 reveals David's heartfelt conviction for the foundation of a life laid bare before God.

> You have searched me, LORD,
>   and you know me.
> You know when I sit and when I rise;
>   you perceive my thoughts from afar.
> You discern my going out and my lying down;
>   you are familiar with all my ways.
> Before a word is on my tongue
>   you, LORD, know it completely.
> You hem me in behind and before,
>   and you lay your hand upon me.

Such knowledge is too wonderful for me,
    too lofty for me to attain.

Where can I go from your Spirit?
    Where can I flee from your presence?
If I go up to the heavens, you are there;
    if I make my bed in the depths, you are there.
If I rise on the wings of the dawn,
    if I settle on the far side of the sea,
even there your hand will guide me,
    your right hand will hold me fast.
If I say, "Surely the darkness will hide me
    and the light become night around me,"
even the darkness will not be dark to you;
    the night will shine like the day,
    for darkness is as light to you.

For you created my inmost being;
    you knit me together in my mother's womb.
I praise you because I am fearfully and wonderfully
        made;
    your works are wonderful,
    I know that full well.
My frame was not hidden from you
    when I was made in the secret place,
    when I was woven together in the depths of the earth.
Your eyes saw my unformed body;
    all the days ordained for me were written in your book
    before one of them came to be.
How precious to me are your thoughts, God!
    How vast is the sum of them!

Were I to count them,
    they would outnumber the grains of sand—
    when I awake, I am still with you.

Psalm 139 teaches us important truths: (1) Our hearts are fully exposed to our all-knowing, all-present, and all-powerful Creator-God and (2) attempts to withhold emotional honesty from God are ultimately futile since all of life, from the womb to the tomb, is underneath His divine observation.

Emotional Honesty

David understood that God's holy line of sight was unlimited. He was convinced there was no place one could travel outside God's gaze, and it would be meaningless to attempt to evade His presence. The only logical choice would be to acknowledge that we are always under God's divine observation and there is always an open invitation to friendship with the God who fearfully made us in love before we could perform for this love. By the end of this verse, most of us press pause on reading the entire chapter, especially in congregational settings. We typically stop short of the verses that will follow, but the subsequent passage holds some important pillars about emotional honesty before God:

- Emotional honesty does not withhold our human complexity from God.
- Emotional honesty is not performative and does not mean telling God what we think He wants to hear.
- Emotional honesty is centered on trust in the safety of God's perfect love.

In the verses that follow, David transitions from a posture of praise into a posture of utter confession. As he pours out the contents of a grieved heart on the heels of poetic prayer, we are reminded that emotional honesty is not a straight line. It is a multi-dimensional, moment-by-moment offering because we, as human beings, have multidimensional, moment-by-moment emotional responses in the daily ebb and flow of life.

> If only you, God, would slay the wicked!
> > Away from me, you who are bloodthirsty!
> They speak of you with evil intent;
> > your adversaries misuse your name.
> Do I not hate those who hate you, LORD,
> > and abhor those who are in rebellion against you?
> I have nothing but hatred for them;
> > I count them my enemies.
> Search me, God, and know my heart;
> > test me and know my anxious thoughts.
> See if there is any offensive way in me,
> > and lead me in the way everlasting.

PSALM 139:19-24

David viewed God as his Shepherd, the One whose sovereign sight was far above his own. His emotional honesty came from the birthplace of trust. In many ways he teaches us that our divine entrustments *from* God will only be dispensed to the extent of our relational trust *in* God. David's emotional honesty was proving ground for the kind of faith that would be strong enough to hold steady throughout the treacherous trajectory of leadership in the years to come.

God had already placed certain qualities and gifts in David, but they would only be matured in the sanctity of private and sincere relationship. Through the practice of emotional honesty, David would develop a level of vulnerability and intimacy with God that would condition his heart to put his confidence not in his abilities but in his God. We see this in 1 Samuel 17:45 as David stands before Goliath:

> David said to the Philistine, "You come against me with
> sword and spear and javelin, but I come against you in
> the name of the LORD Almighty, the God of the armies of
> Israel, whom you have defied."

The faith with which David was able to confront Goliath was a sword sharpened through a million private moments of devotion. In the face of imminent destruction, no amount of training, education, skill, or charisma could impart the supernatural grace and favor required for the impossible to become possible. David appealed not to his physical strength or to the power of his intellect. David appealed to the power of his God, and this level of radical trust overflowed from years of rich relational history with God as a person.

The beauty of the biblical narrative as the living, breathing Word of God is that, in so many ways, the story of one is the story of all of us. Here, millennia later, so much about the world has changed and yet we are alive underneath the same skies that inspired Psalm 19. We breathe the same air David breathed when he wrote Psalm 139. We are sojourners through the same world the fathers and mothers of our faith traveled and trusted through.

Ages later, David's journey of vulnerability in Scripture, along with the psalms he penned, serve as a blueprint giving us permission to allow our unsanitized prayers to reach God's hearing from the overflow of a vulnerable heart. Yes, God is already aware of what is present in the deepest chambers of the human heart, but communication is the difference between relational observation and relational intimacy. I can observe something about someone, but until that person communicates directly with me, I am a peripheral fixture at best. I have not yet been invited to engage with them one-on-one with what I already know. Emotional honesty goes beyond intellectual acknowledgment of God's sovereign knowledge and invites Him in—on a personal level—to engage with the heart. David had his finger on the pulse of this reality in his best and brightest moments.

But we don't always choose right here in the tension of our post-Eden realities, and neither did David. The successes and failures of his life illustrate how relational intimacy with God can be impacted by two primary approaches to emotional honesty. In our relationship with God there are two types of burdens we wrestle with: the burden of silence and the burden of truth telling.

The Burden of Silence

In our choice to remain silent and withhold emotional honesty from God there may be a sense of momentary relief. We may be temporarily spared from having to courageously expend the energy it takes to communicate with full authenticity. We may temporarily avoid having to lay our hearts on the altar of risk. We may retreat instead to our inner safe place, where we can be alone with our thoughts, feelings, and assumptions. While this may feel like a safer route, choosing silence places a burden on the relationship: the burden of disconnection and/or disintegration. When we choose to withhold truth, this always and eventually accumulates, over time, into relational distance. We are always moving one of two directions in every relationship: closer together or further apart. When we choose a pattern of silence in a relationship, it is only a matter of time before we find ourselves gravitating toward isolation and, eventually, emotional exile. Confession involves the act of entrusting God with our true emotions. Certain moments of David's life, which we will discuss in this chapter, serve as a cautionary tale as to what can happen when we withhold our feelings from God. This leads us to the second type of burden.

The Burden of Truth Telling

In the burden of truth telling, we feel the weight of words we simply do not want to say out loud, and we wrestle with the tension of our own reluctance to confess the truth even while we know the truth must be said for our own health and the health of the relationship. It is the truth that sets us free (John 8:32). When we choose emotional honesty with God, we are choosing trust—trust in His loving character and trust in His commitment not to abandon the work of His hands. Ultimately we are trusting in His supernatural power to intervene through the power of our own confession. In telling the truth, we loosen the grip of silence and the emotional harm of disintegration, and we move toward relational connectivity and integration with Him. We acknowledge that God already has a sovereign line of sight that includes the landscape of our hearts. In engaging with Him honestly, we are simply inviting His presence into our process to do what no man can do. And when we do this, we discover, to our delight, that God does not feel burdened, as we do, by the weight of our truth. He welcomes the entire contents of our hearts. His yoke is easy and His burden is light (Matthew 11:30), and this is the freedom He extends to us when we come to tell the truth before His throne of grace.

David's life is a case study in the intricacies of both types of burdens and the results of both approaches. We see what occurs in his heart and life when he chooses the burden of silence in 2 Samuel 11:2-5:

> One evening David got up from his bed and walked around on the roof of the palace. From the roof he saw a woman bathing. The woman was very beautiful, and David sent someone to find out about her. The man said, "She is Bathsheba, the daughter of Eliam and the wife of Uriah the Hittite." Then David sent messengers to get her. She came to him, and he slept with her. (Now she was purifying herself from her monthly uncleanness.) Then she went back home. The woman conceived and sent word to David, saying, "I am pregnant."

In this passage we see the result of David's choice to avoid emotional honesty when confronted with the weight of his primal urges. I often wonder how God would have met David in his desire for Bathsheba if he had warred with his flesh before God and won that battle in the sanctum of confession. What would've happened had he withheld his petition to send for Bathsheba and instead brought the truth about his desires and thoughts to God and safe people? What would've been the result of his emotional honesty?

There are some things God won't save us from. Temptation in the skin we live in is one of them. But would David have been saved from his failure? Would he have been empowered by the Spirit to do right before God and walk in the fear of the Lord had he rejected the burden of silence? Without knowing the full depth of his conversations with God, these are hypothetical questions outside the realm of our ability to assess in the here and now, but one thing remains true: The enemy deals in deceit. What lies does the enemy whisper when we feel conflicted about emotional honesty with God?

> *Is God's love really strong enough to cover the admission of this temptation, struggle, or sin?*
> *What will happen if the whole truth is confessed?*

The enemy has always used doubt as a strategy to get us to question God's perfect love and authority, ever since he deceived Eve in the Garden with "Did God really say . . . ?" (Genesis 3:1). In the same spirit of curiosity, I wonder what could have happened if Eve had run from the snake and confessed her encounter with temptation. What might've been had she chosen to entertain a conversation with God instead of entertaining a conversation with the enemy?

This brings an important truth to our attention. In the face of temptation, the rejection of silence is a weapon wielded against Satan's snares. When we cast off the burden of silence, we engage with a God who has the power to help us resist the enemy and watch him flee. We appeal to a God who can flood the darkness of secrets with the light of His truth and love. In a homesick world where we are exposed to the realities of the enemy, the flesh, and the world, we must operate in sobriety, aware of what leads to failure to emotionally connect with God. Paul Tripp gives us twelve things that lead to God "amnesia":

anger
control
discontent
doubt
drivenness
entitlement

envy
exhaustion
fear
relational dysfunction
self-centeredness
spiritual coldness[1]

There is wisdom in examining our hearts for the presence of these invisible enemies since all of them are branches from a tree rooted in what it means to live as a human being moving through a post-Eden world.

And yet, sin nature and surrender to temptation aren't the only reasons we reject emotional honesty. Our inability to tell the truth in the face of danger or harm of any kind often has a root system that was planted in the soil of our origin stories.

Getting at the Root

I remember where I was when I first learned that emotional honesty was a choice I would have to make at my own risk. This belief found its origins on the back roads of a small West Texas town when I was a child. My older brother and I visited extended family over several weeks of summer vacation every year, and this always catapulted my preadolescent brain and body into the deep end of insecurity. On the surface, summers in West Texas were a mix of cherry limeades, hide-and-seek, pink-ombré sunsets, and the lingering smell of oil wells. But I always felt the nagging weight and darkness of a low-humming anxiety. I never felt as safe and secure during these summer weeks as I felt in my own home. I was a certifiable introvert whose life orbited around the nucleus of the Mexican mission I was raised in. I was a loner outside that context, and I didn't prefer change. I was the kid who asked for the same lunch in the same lunch box every day. Predictability was security for me. I was a creature of habit. Leaving the security of home for a host of unknowns shook the foundations of my unstable, preteen inner world. One day a tsunami of anxiety sank my heart underwater as a family member drove me and my older brother to a destination that triggered all my worst fears. I was expected to wear a swimsuit. Like many little girls, my childhood had been riddled with body shame. I was teased mercilessly for not being a size zero, and I had learned to protect myself from ridicule through self-preservation. I had a PhD in avoidance and escapism. My systems of control were locked and loaded on every level of life to prevent being confronted with the face of scorn. I was held captive by a fear of rejection.

As if the complexity of my own internal flood of emotions wasn't enough, I was being escorted into this situation with an extended family member who had a reputation for being fiery tempered. I knew the possibility of a compassionate response was slim to none. I made every attempt to cauterize my emotions, but the pain could not be silenced. As we neared our destination, I could no longer hold back my tears. A subtle sniffle turned into a quiet cry, and before I knew it, I was weeping loudly. I was ten years old when she turned around and raged at me, demanding I stop crying at once. Anger. Threats. Dismissal. Shame. I felt unprotected and alone. My takeaways? *You're too much. It's not safe to cry. No one is coming to rescue you. Telling the truth is too risky.* This was the day I learned that it was easier to keep my emotions in a vault. This was the day I learned that emotional honesty wasn't a right but a privilege, a privilege that (I thought) was not available to someone like me.

How many stories like this exist? How many of us have been shamed for our God-given emotions and told it's unacceptable, immature, unholy, or weak to be human, authentic, and honest?

The reality is that once we've lived through these relational woundings, many of us place the template of our harmful human experiences on our relationship with our loving God. Our horizontal relationships condition us to believe we simply do not have permission to be wholly truthful with God without the risk of rejection.

The tension we feel around being emotionally honest with God can be quelled when we consider these truths:

- God's divine nature testifies to a love that covers a multitude of sins.
- The biblical narrative is a story of God's faithfulness to an unfaithful people. From the Garden of Eden to the garden of Gethsemane and the table set before us in eternity, God longs for relationship with His children.
- The Kingdom is not a transactional institution—it is a family.

The voice in our heads that tells us to withhold emotional honesty from God may reverberate off the walls of our hearts in Mom's or Dad's or Grandpa's or Grandma's voice. Someone handed us the first brick to build a fortress around our hearts. We then learned how to build the wall, inch by inch, year by year, relationship by relationship. The rest, as they say, is history . . . but it doesn't have to be.

Human relationships are complex. A walls-down, heart-open mentality isn't safe in every room. There's wisdom in being as wise as serpents and as harmless as doves in horizontal relationships (Matthew 10:16). The problem enters when we apply our storied trauma in this area to a God who longs to befriend us. Dr. Dan Allender helps us understand how previous trauma can inform our present availability to God's love: "When you use the past to create a life in the present that is not open to the kindness, tenderness, grace, [and] mercy of God, you have in some ways used the past to form the future based on a commitment to self-protection."[2] The unhealed wounds in our story can indeed limit our experience of the God who fearfully made us in our mothers' wombs and who knows the number of hairs on our heads. The God who offers a perfect love that covers a multitude of sins.

We may experience these limitations through two primary emotions that serve as obstacles to choosing relational integration with God: pride and fear.

Pride is at the root of any desire to remain autonomous from God and to withhold love, honor, communication, and connection. When we do this knowingly—choosing autonomy from God—it is rebellion. But many of us do this unknowingly. We place life in categories that we either grant or deny God access to. *I will choose what I want to share with God and bring to Him only the parts of me I want to communicate to Him.* Both of these approaches are ultimately rooted in pride.

Fear is why we find it so difficult to present ourselves to God as we truly are. We fear judgment. We're afraid of rejection. We're afraid for a world of reasons. God is holy; we are not. We recall Romans 3:10 (ESV)—"None is righteous, no, not one"—and despair. A measure of distrust is at play, an inability to trust in God's mercy, forgiveness, and transformative resurrection power.

In their book *The Relational Soul,* counselor Richard Plass and spiritual director James Cofield speak to this reality: "Scripture tells the story of a loving God taking the initiative to restore our capacity for intimacy. It is the story of God overcoming our self-absorbed mistrust."[3]

While David had moments of spiritual collapse, he didn't always get it wrong. In fact, God called him "a man after my own heart" (Acts 13:22) because David frequently chose right. We see this in Psalm 25, a passage of Scripture near and dear to me. As a child who felt relationally vacant outside of church life, this was the psalm I would read in the watches of the night when I felt the sting of isolation the most. The emotionally honest words of David would wash over me. In the presence of God through these words, I was alone but not lonely.

Turn to me and be gracious to me,
    for I am lonely and afflicted.
Relieve the troubles of my heart
    and free me from my anguish.
Look on my affliction and my distress
    and take away all my sins.
See how numerous are my enemies
    and how fiercely they hate me!

Guard my life and rescue me;
    do not let me be put to shame,
    for I take refuge in you.
May integrity and uprightness protect me,
    because my hope, LORD, is in you.

Deliver Israel, O God,
    from all their troubles!
PSALM 25:16-22

These verses became the stuff of my childhood midnight prayers and gave me full permission to present the complex universe of my heart to God. Night after night I discovered the weight of my humanity and the burden of my experience was no match for God's strong arm and His beautiful, relational invitation.

David's emotional honesty with God taught me one foundational truth: God prioritizes relationship. It's at the center of His heart. Scripture reveals the emotional range of a God who is compassionate, loving, and kind while also illustrating His capacity for righteous jealousy, anger, and grief. We have been made in the image of a God who feels. We begin to see it in the halls of Old Testament history and watch it crescendo in the life and times of Jesus, Emmanuel—God with us. Jesus, fully God and fully man, stooped down low to experience the full range of human emotion, from the depths of our despair to the height of our joy.

"Jesus wept" (John 11:35), and He gives us permission to weep too. Tears of mourning, longing, sadness, and grief. Tears of gratitude, response, joy, and laughter. The Son of David taught us what David knew: There's a place for the entirety of who we are in our secret place with God. Sometimes—when I can't speak or sing—tears become worship because they are an emotionally honest response. Sometimes tears and tears alone are a love language to God. The next time you feel inclined to weep, don't withhold those tears. Allow them to flow, and know that no one is a better caretaker of the human heart than the One who made yours. He welcomes your tears. Every part of you is safe in His sight.

We have been made in the image of a God who is a master in complexity. He is the conductor in the symphony of all things in the seen and the unseen world. If He can hem in the borders of the oceans and set the constellations in their place, if He can order the rhythms of the sun and moon, if He holds all things together in an estimated one hundred million galaxies,[4] He knows how to navigate the complex landscape in the universe of the human heart. God is not intimidated or discouraged by our complexity when we openly entrust Him with it. He is the master of mystery.

The Bible helps us see our own stories in the stories of the fathers and mothers of our faith, and if we desire to replace our view of God as a concept with the intimacy of relating to God as a person, we must walk in the footsteps of the psalmist. We must accept God's invitation into a continuous awareness of His activity and personhood in real time. This looks like a vertically aligned life, where our hearts are continuously aimed upward to hear and know God's voice. This is a space where there is no end but a perpetual flow of intimacy, where the Great I AM is in every conversation, every blade of grass, every blooming flower, and every question and nuance of the human experience. A place where His presence is personal, from midnight to morning and every moment in between. This is the invitation of God—nothing less.

Reflection Questions

1. How does David's emotional range in Psalm 139 give us permission to pray emotionally honest prayers?

2. Which do you most identify with in your life with God: the burden of silence or the burden of truth telling? Is your answer storied?

3. What can we learn from David's moral collapse, and how can we protect ourselves, on a spiritual level, from temptation?

4. What are some practical ways you can develop a vertically aligned life with God, a life that produces a continuous flow of intimacy and conversation with Him?

THE FREEDOM OF SURRENDER

Finding Hope in Letting Go

In the fall of 2021, I was asked to consider teaching on Mary, the mother of Jesus, for an Advent series at a church in the Chicago area. Having grown up in the Hispanic Christian tradition and having heard all the Nativity stories as a child, I can tell you this task felt daunting. Sure, I knew who Mary was, but I didn't *really* know who Mary was. My knowledge of her as the mother of Jesus was peripheral and anecdotal at best. In the Hispanic tradition, Mary is frequently revered as an untouchable icon. I had yet to darken the door of her humanity and had certainly not taken a deep dive into the depth of treasures her life and story held.

So I committed to study Mary for six weeks leading up to my teaching commitment. As I read through her story, I was surprised by the kindredness I began to feel. Mary was plucked out of obscurity. So was I. She was a young, unknown, unmarried girl from the middle of nowhere. I grew up in a tiny Texas town famous only for its 4A varsity football team and its yearly polka festival. Mary was seen by God. Somehow, despite all my unlikeliness, this always remained intact, internally, for me as well.

God was the wind behind my back in the sunrise of life as I walked through the tall green grass in my yellow dress at eighteen months old. He was the soft Presence I could be sure of when I laid my little head down to rest after a fourteen-hour day watching my parents save the world in our Mexican mission. He settled my angsty teenage heart when my hands played the piano for altar call, as I watched our beloved people reach for the help of an eternal hand. He was my best friend in every lonely hallway, every quiet birthday, and every empty Friday night. I had been born into great disruption and great obscurity, a space where life would be void of harmony and presence without God Himself. I couldn't see it then, but my aloneness with God would become the most important key to my own spiritual formation.

I wouldn't know how to secure many things the world deemed significant: money, success, power, praise. But I *would* know how to find God Himself in any room I walked into. This was the gift of all gifts that would define who I was and who I would become. In the universe of my heart God was the sun, the moon, and the stars. His light would flood the dark. His glory would fill the void. But it was God's soft spot for the underdog that most endeared me to His heart. It would take a lifetime to begin to understand that God's value of the unlikely wasn't just aimed in my direction; it is the heart posture He has always taken in response to flawed human power dynamics.

In the encounter between the angel Gabriel and Mary in Luke 1:26-35, we see evidence of God resisting human power structures and choosing the least likely.

In the sixth month of Elizabeth's pregnancy, God sent the angel Gabriel to Nazareth, a town in Galilee, to a virgin pledged to be married to a man named Joseph, a descendant of David. The virgin's name was Mary. The angel went to her and said, "Greetings, you who are highly favored! The Lord is with you."

Mary was greatly troubled at his words and wondered what kind of greeting this might be. But the angel said to her, "Do not be afraid, Mary; you have found favor with God. You will conceive and give birth to a son, and you are to call him Jesus. He will be great and will be called the Son of the Most High. The Lord God will give him the throne of his father David, and he will reign over Jacob's descendants forever; his kingdom will never end."

"How will this be," Mary asked the angel, "since I am a virgin?"

The angel answered, "The Holy Spirit will come on you, and the power of the Most High will overshadow you. So the holy one to be born will be called the Son of God."

Gabriel refers to Mary, an unwed, unknown young woman as "highly favored" and tells her, "The Lord is with you." The Greek word for "favor" here is from *charis*—which means unmerited, undeserved grace from God. What Gabriel is describing is God's grace. There is favor marking Mary's life because God's presence is flowing from His grace and into this moment of divine chosenness. It is not money, power, appearance, or any other cultural qualifiers that mark Mary's life with God's approval. The purity of God's presence has set her apart for this appointed moment of encounter with divine destiny.

Mary's inclusion in God's redemptive story was not a product of the world's standards of eligibility for honor. In that time and place, power was systemic and male-centric. There was not yet a Messiah who granted personal access to God. There were a temple, a sacrificial system, a priesthood, and a religious calendar. As an unmarried teenager and a woman, Mary lived outside these structures. Even still, God gazed down on her lowly state and saw the purity of Mary's heart. In the opening lines of her song in Luke 1, we see Mary marveling at her unlikeliness and operating in full sobriety of who she appeared to be to the world around her. Yet she did not choose to disqualify herself; instead, she embraced surrender. She decided to trust God's choice of her regardless of how misaligned it was with man's standards of eligibility.

And Mary said:

> "My soul glorifies the Lord
>   and my spirit rejoices in God my Savior,
> for he has been mindful
>   of the humble state of his servant.
> From now on all generations will call me blessed,
>   for the Mighty One has done great things for me—
>   holy is his name.
> His mercy extends to those who fear him,
>   from generation to generation.
> He has performed mighty deeds with his arm;
>   he has scattered those who are proud in their inmost
>   thoughts.
> He has brought down rulers from their thrones
>   but has lifted up the humble.
> He has filled the hungry with good things
>   but has sent the rich away empty.

He has helped his servant Israel,
>
> remembering to be merciful
>
> to Abraham and his descendants forever,
>
> just as he promised our ancestors."

LUKE 1:46-55

Mary's song isn't just a beautiful moment in Scripture; it also reflects God's heart and is a personal act of surrender. As I took the opportunity to study this passage, her words seemed to resonate on a neurobiological level as I read them, in part, through the grid of my own origin story. "He has been mindful of the humble state of his servant. . . . He has scattered those who are proud in their inmost thoughts." There are some who choose humility later in life because of being brought to their knees through moments of reckoning, and then there are those of us who had early exposure to formational fires that marked us with meekness. Humility opposes pride and entitlement, and humility was the cornerstone of my childhood missional community due to our socioeconomic challenges. Mary was also born into humility through the crucible of unlikeliness. She was anything but primed for positional power by the standards of her time. We have enough scriptural evidence to assume that the religious leaders, in their conflated view of their own dominion and authority, would never have permitted someone as lowly as Mary to be given such a holy role, a role laced with implications of immense privilege, divine favor, and spiritual authority.

Yet every person in every chapter of the Bible befriended God at the intersection of their earthly disqualifications and His sovereign choice. Why would God give preference to the last and the least? Perhaps one dimension of this multidimensional conversation revolves around relational dependence. If the biblical narrative and the headlines of our time have taught us anything, it is this truth: Power without the fear of the Lord always and eventually leads to corruption. And the fear of the Lord is radical loyalty to God, which is relational at its root. A life of the fear of the Lord orbits around honoring Him. Scripture clearly identifies Mary as a person who lived this kind of life.

Surrendering to God, Even When We Don't Understand

Mary's story gives us a window into what can happen when God's values and His choice supersede the values and choices of a broken and homesick world. Mary was highly favored despite her unlikeliness in the world's eyes, but the irony of it all wasn't in her cultural ineligibility but in the fact that Mary herself was the first person to question God's choice of her.

Luke 1:29 says, "Mary was greatly troubled at his words and wondered what kind of greeting this might be."

The word rendered "greatly troubled" is *diatarassō*, which means "thoroughly stirred up," "confused," or "perplexed."

Have you ever been thrown off by a calling that felt far beyond your own dreams? So fantastical and seemingly out of reach that you were utterly perplexed? Most days of my life, since God called me to ministry at age sixteen, have felt this way. *Are you sure, God?* Mary must have wondered what God might be doing as well. The word translated "wondered" in Luke 1:29 is *dialogizomai*, which refers to the use of logic or reasoning. Mary was intensely pondering how God's call on her life could be true.

"'How will this be,' Mary asked the angel, 'since I am a virgin?'" (Luke 1:34).

Could the root sentiment of her question have been "Are you sure you want me to do this?" or maybe "How could you ask me to do this?" I have personally experienced this subtle but important difference. There is indeed a spectrum of bewilderment when God asks you to do something that is far beyond your own limitations. If I were Mary, I would've been asking these questions. In fact, though our circumstances have been vastly different, I *have* asked these questions: *God, do you know you're sending me out into a world that might reject me? Do you know you're sending me into situations where others might misunderstand my call? Could you consider sending someone with more worldly qualifications?*

It is not a sin to present God with our desire to understand. Amid being perplexed, Mary openly asked a logical question. She fully understood the limitations of her cultural status. And this moment in the story is a great reminder that God often does the miraculous in our lives not despite our limitations but *because* of our limitations. This is where His glory and power are revealed. The angel answers her question with the words "Nothing will be impossible with God" (Luke 1:37, NET).

Mary received a response and reached a moment of decision. She was faced with the magnitude of her own unlikeliness and the reality of God's call. Writer and theologian Thomas Merton says, "Sooner or later, if we follow Christ we have to risk everything in order to gain everything. We have to gamble on the invisible and risk all that we see and taste and feel. But we know the risk is worth it, because there is nothing more insecure than the transient world."[1]

There's a difference between reckless abandon set in motion by a selfish agenda and radical faith fueled by a divine encounter. Mary enters radical faith when she says, "Yes, I am a servant of the Lord; let this happen to me according to your word" (Luke 1:38, NET).

And this is where we come to our central focus in Mary's incredible story: surrender.

Mary's story illustrates three things surrender accomplishes in our own spiritual formation and life with God:

1. *Surrender dethrones the idols of the heart.* Mary surrendered. Even though she was wide-eyed and operating in full sobriety of her limitations. Since she was an unmarried teenager, it was extremely likely she would be misjudged and mislabeled as unfit and unqualified. Even still, she chose to operate out of God's favor rather than fight for man's commendation. For one moment, try to fathom the depths of this kind of radical loyalty to God. I wonder if He knew that the idols of man's approval and cultural good standing had not yet hypnotized her heart. Perhaps she had learned to live in the world without being defined by it.

   Mary took her place in a long line of fathers and mothers of the faith who walked in the fear of the Lord and loved God's Kingdom right . . . to the extent that worldly idols of the heart were crushed underneath the weight of the reality of God Himself. Mary's loyalty to God as a person was her priority, and she surrendered to the sovereignty, mystery, and activity of God at all costs.

2. *Surrender develops durability in the fragile places of our hearts and stories.* Mary's fragile heart grew to fit the size of a brave calling that would endure the tension of the world, the flesh, and the enemy. When Jesus was presented in the Temple and Simeon told Mary "a sword will pierce your own soul too" (Luke 2:35), this was a telling moment. Over time God would cultivate Mary's durability to persevere in

loving, protecting, and caring for the child meant to save a world He'd spoken into being but would never fully belong in. Her heart would be pierced in the process.

Mary would survive the heartache on the road back to Jerusalem only to find her missing twelve-year-old son in the Temple. Twenty-one years later she would be granted the strength to stand at a cross and watch her son bear the unbearable weight of a calling she was obedient to bring Him into the world to face. She would learn to trust God through decades of mystery as she sat in the waiting room of trust. Things wouldn't make total sense until the Resurrection and Ascension. She would spend years living in the tension of the now and the not yet.

Mary was in a long line of faithful pilgrims who knew this world was not their home and who gave their whole hearts and full sacrificial yes to follow the current of what the late great Rich Mullins referred to as "the reckless raging fury / that they call the love of God."[2]

If you're reading this today and you have said yes to God, you can know with confidence that there is a great cloud of witnesses who have surrendered to the current of the force of God's will, a will you and I sometimes find it so difficult to yield to. Take heart. There is a great cloud of witnesses who undoubtedly loved and lost big, took risks and failed, grew cynical and later recovered their faith.

I thank God for followers of Jesus who choose to lose their life to find it. I thank God for those who, for the eternal joy set before them, surrender to bear their own crosses (Hebrews 12:2) because they know their reward is not in this life. Mary lost her life to discover it and, for the joy set before her, she became durable in fragile places. Sons and daughters like this have their eyes set on an eternal horizon. Hebrews 11 tells us the world is not worthy of them, the ones who have laid their best plans on the altar of costly surrender. We see the supernatural overshadow the natural through this process of trust and childlike faith, time and time again. This was Mary's life, and the same power that flowed through the complexity of her story is available to you and me.

3. *Surrender releases us from the bondage of our need for control and into the intimacy of radical dependence and trust.* Mary questioned the impossible and then surrendered to and endured it. She yielded to the formative activity of God. Mary was not forming herself; she was being formed. She relinquished control. For those who wrestle with the test of surrender, control is the dopamine hit of choice. Yet often the more control we secure the more we feel the hollowness of our own independence from God. Our control doesn't satisfy us on a soul level. Even when it results in achievement or success, it is not the salve our souls seek. Control begets control, keeping us enslaved to a formula that binds our souls—on a spiritual level—in a cycle that prevents us from living in true freedom. Our surrender to God Himself positions us for the possibility of being surprised by an all-knowing, all-powerful, and all-present God.

I had to wait until my late twenties to walk through a season of my own life in which I experienced a level of surrender to God that marked me in a before-and-after way.

In truth, this story was years in the making—a slow, controlled burn. Throughout adolescence, my life had been littered with endless trips to the doctor. After many years of mysterious symptoms with no diagnosis, I was told at the age of nineteen that I would never be able to conceive a child. I remember the day I walked into the doctor's office in downtown Dallas to hear this news. The doctor read my chart, looked up, and said, "You will never be able to have children, unless . . ." Then he pointed upward. "Unless . . . God." At the time, those words landed on an ambivalent heart. I was young, unattached, and had zero dreams of ever becoming a wife and mother. My life revolved around music and ministry. I was utterly committed to my calling and moved with undistracted intention toward the fullness of God's missional plan for my life. I left the office that day relatively unfazed. A loss is only a loss when the hope of the human heart hangs in the balance. I had yet to have a reason to become emotionally invested in the possibility of motherhood.

As the years passed, God blessed my dedication to my calling. My music bloomed. I moved to Nashville after winning a national songwriting award. Like Mary, I had been plucked out of obscurity by God, and the invitation was bigger than my aspirations. The invitation wasn't just to become a songwriter. The invitation was to enter a full-fledged developmental path as an artist, a path led by a few music-industry veterans I deeply respected. A year into this beautifully life-consuming process, I met a boy. He was kind, handsome, and a Tennessee native. We became fast friends, but his ability to lead and challenge me as a strong-willed, independent Latina was the trait that wooed me. New music was in the air, but wedding bells weren't far behind. We were introduced in January, engaged by June, and married by late August. They say when you know, you know. The girl who had zero plans to be a wife was fully surprised by God when He brought not only a husband but also a whirlwind love story.

My dreams expanded as our love grew, and suddenly my heart began to feel the tension of my health diagnosis. As I looked at my blue-eyed, blond-haired husband, I felt the ache of longing awaken in me for the first time. I would likely never have a little blond-haired, blue-eyed baby to hold. I would likely never know what it meant to stare back into the face of someone who was half me and half the love of my life. As couples around us began to conceive, we received baby shower invitation after baby shower invitation. Isolation set in. The world around us moved forward, and we remained stuck in a painful holding pattern. The air is thick in the waiting room between the *now* and the *not yet*.

As years passed, the dream of a child never departed from our hearts, but in the fall of 2006, I managed to allow my heart to hope for a positive pregnancy test only to wake up to devastating news that led to another month of open-ended grief. In my sorrow I went back to bed and cried myself to sleep. I wanted to take the edge off facing the reality the waking world held for me. As I drifted off to sleep, the Lord gave me a dream. It wasn't just any kind of dream. It wasn't a visitation from an angel, but it felt supernaturally charged.

I dreamt I was driving through a lush, green residential area in a familiar but distant location. I drove through what seemed like futuristic streets and turned onto a side street and into a brick duplex. I parked in the driveway. As I walked up to the home, I passed a window through which I saw a beautiful brown-haired, brown-eyed girl washing dishes over the kitchen sink. She had long, straight hair. She looked like me and she looked like my husband. I woke up from the dream in tears. And although I had no way of knowing the future in that moment, I felt comforted by God, as a child is comforted by their mother.

A few years went by, and during this season I did two things:

(1) I accepted what I could not control and I grieved with hope and (2) I invested my time in seeking God through prayer and engaging with Him in inner healing work.

I committed to attend an out-of-state retreat where the focus was on engaging in the work of forgiveness and receiving Christ's love. During this time, God revealed what was truly in my heart as I traversed the valley of all that could not be controlled or understood even as I watched others escape it. I remember where I was when the stirring in my heart sounded like *Tanya, you don't believe I love you as much as I love other people. You believe that if I truly loved you, then you would have what other people have.*

I burst into tears of relief. This was the revelation I had traveled three states to receive. There was not one ounce of condemnation in these words, only loving care. This is what the voice of our Father sounds like. The irony of these words was in the timing. I heard them just as the facilitators were playing the Crucifixion scene in *The Passion of the Christ*. My heart broke open at the reality that God could never have loved me more than He did at that very moment, when He sacrificed His own Son on the cross so that I could experience His relationship-first care.

Our response to the invitation of surrender will set us on one of two trajectories: We will either move closer to God or further away. Over the years my heart had grown protective. Tenderness had been exchanged for firm attempts to control. But now I was softening to God. I was softening to the idea of trust.

As I returned home and this season progressed, God began to bring Ecclesiastes 3 to my heart in recurring fashion. It was everywhere. When I turned on the ignition in my car, the radio played, "To everything (turn, turn, turn) / There is a season (turn, turn, turn) . . ."[3] When I flipped on the TV, a popular sitcom was playing this same song. I saw an excerpt from Ecclesiastes 3 on a black-and-white billboard. I heard it in sermons. It was a perpetual refrain. I knew God was trying to tell me something. His activity around this passage of Scripture was undeniable.

> For everything there is a season, and a time for every
> matter under heaven:
>
> > a time to be born, and a time to die;
> > a time to plant, and a time to pluck up what is planted;
> > a time to kill, and a time to heal;
> > a time to break down, and a time to build up;
> > a time to weep, and a time to laugh;
> > a time to mourn, and a time to dance;
> > a time to cast away stones, and a time to gather stones
> > together;
> > a time to embrace, and a time to refrain from embracing;
> > a time to seek, and a time to lose;
> > a time to keep, and a time to cast away;
> > a time to tear, and a time to sew;
> > a time to keep silence, and a time to speak;
> > a time to love, and a time to hate;
> > a time for war, and a time for peace.

ECCLESIASTES 3:1-8, ESV

Through prayer and discernment, the message became clear: No season is final. Every winter always eventually turns into spring. I didn't know if these words would result in a change in my situation, but I knew how to discern the activity of God, and I knew my questions were under divine observation. I knew God had His eye on me, and in the darkness of uncertainty, He was offering me the light of His presence and inviting me to surrender my fears.

I became well acquainted with sorrow and mystery during this season. I can also confess that, as I write this book, there are still unsolved mysteries present in my story now. But I want you to know that three months after God opened Ecclesiastes 3 to me, He also opened my womb to defy the odds and supernaturally intervene in our war with infertility.

Like Mary, I had been invited by God to trade all my plans for the possibility of being surprised by Him. Mary's invitation came through an angel; mine had come through a dream. The beautiful, long-haired brunette I saw in that dream looks identical to my precious fifteen-year-old daughter today. If that isn't miraculous enough, she also has a younger brother. Miracle baby number two is eleven. He is a carbon copy of yours truly with his dad's love of all things mechanical. My pregnancy with him was also announced through a prophetic dream. I can't explain why these things happen. All I can tell you is that the God of the Old Testament and the New Testament has a way of jumping off the pages of Scripture and entering our stories in real time. I have two real-life miracles in my home to prove it.

When we choose surrender, we leave room for God to write a better story. We make space for the possibility of joy. In Luke 1:47 Mary says, "My spirit rejoices in God my Savior." Joy was the result of Mary's surrender. But I'm not referring to the finite, fictional definition of *joy*. We're not talking about a euphoric, emotional experience absent of earthly tension or worldly grief. We are talking about a both/and kind of joy. A joy that makes space for all the love and the tension we all know follows full surrender. Mary's logical question was a validation of the tension to come, and yet she accepted the call because she believed God was the final, conclusive authority over all things.

Joy is about belongingness. It's about knowing God as our

permanent home. Mary's security was not in her likeliness. Her security was in the safety of a friendship with God, and because she believed He was trustworthy, she was released from the bondage of control and carried on God's divine current into the fullness of all she was created to be. She willingly surrendered her plans, and this radical surrender positioned her to live into a story that would change the world and spiritually form her into the likeness of the One she was miraculously called to bear. When God calls, His ability to appoint and anoint outweighs the criteria of the culture and the natural methods and systems of this world. The Holy Spirit overshadowed Mary so that the natural became supernatural. I wonder what it would look like if we allowed the Holy Spirit to overshadow our natural abilities so God's supernatural power could flow through us. Could we have the kind of humility to ask for that? Could we have the humility to seek the face of God before we consult the wisdom of man?

Mary was willing to make space in her life to be overshadowed. She was willing to cultivate room for the miraculous. What might God be asking you to surrender? What task might He be calling you to that unearths your own sense of unlikeliness? May we have the childlike faith to answer as Mary answered: "I am the Lord's servant. . . . May your word to me be fulfilled" (Luke 1:38).

Reflection Questions

1. What did Mary have to overcome to say yes to the fullness of God's call?

2. What are the idols of the culture we have been set in that have a personal bearing on our willingness to surrender?

3. What would it look like to choose consecration and obedience in these areas so that we can surrender more fully?

4. The invitation of God is to trust, not control. What are some spiritual and practical ways you can posture your heart to lean into this space with Him?

THE SECRET PLACE

Finding God in Obscurity

Imagine being born into a divine call from God Himself, a call that involved a holy visitation from an angelic messenger and an invitation into a life destined to change the course of history. Consider what it would be like to be filled with the Holy Spirit even in your mother's womb and to grow up knowing your purpose was to prepare the way for another person to become the hero in the story. Luke 1 gives us deeper context for John the Baptist's life of consecration and the first stirrings that led to his supernatural insertion in the redemptive story of God.

> The angel said to him, "Do not be afraid, Zechariah,
> for your prayer has been heard, and your wife Elizabeth
> will bear you a son, and you shall call his name John.
> And you will have joy and gladness, and many will
> rejoice at his birth, for he will be great before the Lord.
> And he must not drink wine or strong drink, and

he will be filled with the Holy Spirit, even from his
mother's womb. And he will turn many of the children
of Israel to the Lord their God, and he will go before
him in the spirit and power of Elijah, to turn the hearts
of the fathers to the children, and the disobedient to
the wisdom of the just, to make ready for the Lord a
people prepared."

LUKE 1:13-17, ESV

John the Baptist was sent to live into a supernaturally charged
life, a life that would never be about his name, his reputation,
his dreams, his desires or preferences. His life would only ever be
about the God dream he was chosen for before he could even take
his first breath. John the Baptist was destined for a life untethered
from the world and tethered to God Himself.

The word of God came to John son of Zechariah
in the wilderness. He went into all the country around
the Jordan, preaching a baptism of repentance for the
forgiveness of sins. As it is written in the book of the
words of Isaiah the prophet:

> "A voice of one calling in the wilderness,
> 'Prepare the way for the Lord,
>   make straight paths for him.
> Every valley shall be filled in,
>   every mountain and hill made low.
> The crooked roads shall become straight,
>   the rough ways smooth.
> And all people will see God's salvation.'"

LUKE 3:2-6

Wilderness. This would be the birthplace of John the Baptist's spiritual formation. He would be uniquely and radically positioned for the gift of obscurity with God in the Jordan wilderness, where the River Jordan flows into the Dead Sea. It begins at six hundred feet below sea level and ends at thirteen hundred feet below sea level. One Bible commentator calls it a "hot, uninhabited depression which is wild in every way and removed from all civilization."[1]

John the Baptist would not grow into spiritual maturity or the size of God's singularly important call in the city center under the supervision of religious leaders. The fire within him would be lit and sustained by the Holy Spirit. He was under the influence of God Himself. He would not walk the crowded streets craving integration into society by trade or gifting; he would walk with the Great I Am alone in consecration. He would not feast at the tables of kings and royalty; he would meet the dawn of every day in holy dependence, his eyes aimed upward and into the wild. John the Baptist did not belong to the world. He was God's beloved, sent to fulfill God's Kingdom agenda on His divine timeline.

I wonder what it was like for John to grow up knowing his destiny was crucial to God's plan to save the world. The weight of this level of calling could only be sustained (and intimately directed) by the Great Shepherd Himself. John the Baptist was destined for wilderness, obscurity, suffering, and preparing the way for Jesus, the Messiah, only so he could get out of the way for Him. And he did this faithfully as he modeled what it meant to lay down his life in one long descent into humility and submission. He would be required to live and move and breathe in a wilderness union with God.

We read in Matthew 3:4-6: "John's clothes were made of camel's hair, and he had a leather belt around his waist. His food was locusts and wild honey. People went out to him from Jerusalem and all Judea and the whole region of the Jordan. Confessing their sins, they were baptized by him in the Jordan River."

John lived in full dependence on God, a lifestyle foreshadowing the long descent of Jesus from heaven to a homesick world and his words in Matthew 8:20: "Foxes have dens and birds have nests, but the Son of Man has no place to lay his head."

John the Baptist lived under wilderness stars and sounds and stirrings. He was set apart for a level of consecration that demanded the entirety of his body, soul, and mind. Some might call this radical, but a radical life of consecration has the power to produce a radical level of intimacy with God.

It is no wonder Jesus' commendation of him was "Among those born of women there is no one greater than John" (Luke 7:28). This is a powerful statement, especially when we contrast it with the values of the world we live in. A world that idolizes idealism. The ideal family background, the ideal level of education, the ideal level of experience, the ideal level of influence. These are not new cultural concepts. Man has always defaulted to cultural scripts and hierarchies instead of the purity and simplicity of God's choice and God's ways.

We needn't look further than Jesus Himself to verify this claim. He is described in Acts 4:11 as "the stone [the] builders rejected, which has become the cornerstone." Through the ages our preference for cultural idealism tarnished the purity of biblical alignment in our lives and communities. The pure in heart overlooked for the one who has the best résumé or the best image. The meek and humble overshadowed by the charismatic and popular. Many a kingdom in this day and age does not resemble the Kingdom of God when policies and procedures are less infused with biblical truths and more diluted by business policies and cultural scripts.

John the Baptist's life illustrates the dichotomy between God's priorities and the ways of the world.

I've asked myself one question over the last few years, as mainstream cultural norms have increasingly infiltrated traditional, biblically centered circles. My question is this: *When is the purity of the presence of God in a person's life going to be enough?* In other words, when is God's choice of an individual yielded to His Spirit and His Word going to suffice? A life consecrated to God, filled with His Spirit, and immersed in the Word are biblical qualifications central to God's heart, and they should be central to ours as we steward relationships, opportunities, teams, and organizations. These time-tested principles never expire in God's heart and line of sight. When is the reality that He has called someone going to be enough to override our cultural biases and human preferences? Have we lost the fear of the Lord concerning this? Have we stopped fighting to partner with God for the purity of His Kingdom come, on earth as it is in heaven? Have we forgotten that His precepts have authority over all things? *Whatever we place our confidence in will eventually define us.* This is an important truth to wrestle with in this cultural moment.

Perhaps God's invitation in the here and now is to return to a conscious reverence for and an intentional alignment with God's upside-down Kingdom and upside-down ways . . . which flow from a radical loyalty to Him, produced in the secret place. How many lives, stories, and callings are waiting to be influenced through our biblical alignment in this? John the Baptist's life brings some timely reminders to the surface as we contemplate the practicalities of this invitation—an invitation that begins and ends with a deeply personal commitment to pursue radical loyalty to God.

Jesus' commendation of John the Baptist has important implications about the power of a life hidden in God and the value of radical loyalty produced in seasons of wilderness obscurity. It's important to note that in the biblical narrative God often calls His children there to grow in intimacy and soul-level dependence. The wilderness has often been the doorway of development to enter the fullness of integration into God's Kingdom plan. Abraham, Moses, Joseph, David, and Paul each had journeys in this vulnerable, open-ended space. And let us not forget that Jesus Himself was led into the wilderness by the Holy Spirit. In the words of Dallas Willard: "It was an important day in my life when at last I understood that if he needed forty days in the wilderness at one point, I very likely could use three or four."[2] We can all benefit from learning to embrace desert places. This is where God does some of His holiest work.

The Trinity Stands in Solidarity with Our Suffering

A few years before I began to write this book, I lay in the darkness, awake past midnight, asking God these questions in my own wilderness season. I was living in one of the most confusing and personal ministry heartaches of my life. I felt caught between the corners of my calling and a new awareness that I would never be fully received in a ministry circle I had once called home. There in the dark, as a familiar worship song poured over me, I wept and prayed. I confessed: *God, they will never fully receive me for who you made me to be. Never. Why have you placed me here?*

What followed my vulnerable and raw admission is one of the most sacred, supernatural experiences I've ever had in my own secret place with God. In a distinctly dark wilderness moment, I felt what could only be described as an overwhelming sense that my Trinitarian God had not only heard me but had stooped down low, across time and space, to comfort me with His Word, with

His experience. He began to fill my mind and heart with moments in Scripture in which He, too, had felt the relational sting of rejection: in Eden, in the events that led to the great Flood, when His people rejected Him to worship the golden calf, and when they rejected him as King upon King Saul's rise to power. The list was long and so very personal. God stood in solidarity with my suffering. He was all too familiar with the taste of relational disappointment. He knew how to drink that cup.

In this moment I felt the palpable presence of Jesus, who as a man of many sorrows was well acquainted with grief. Scenes from His life and countless moments during which He had experienced being misunderstood and scorned instantly flooded my heart. Rejection in His hometown of Nazareth. Constant disapproval, cynicism, and dismissal from the religious elite of His day. His aloneness in Gethsemane when He'd asked His friends to watch and pray. On the cross, when the whole world turned its face away. I wept harder at the memory of every scene. Jesus stood in solidarity with me in the same way God is close to the brokenhearted and the crushed in spirit. My own spirit was filled with a real-time knowing.

The family of God attended to my grief with palpable presence made complete as the Holy Spirit, third person of the Trinity, consoled me in a flood of thought. He took me on a journey of what it means to offer comfort, gently convict, and faithfully guide God's children only to have those promptings dismissed in countless invisible moments our hearts will never bear witness to and our eyes will never see. I was not alone, there in the dark of my own corner of the wilderness. My Trinitarian God befriended me, and I wept because in that moment the level of relational intimacy I felt was more personal, biblical, palpable, and meaningful than what any human being, any song, or any sermon could've imparted to me.

This is the incomparable beauty, intimacy, mystery, and power of the secret place. I worshiped in the wake of this supernatural moment in time with my closest friends, the Trinity, and felt sure God not only heard me but had me. The years that followed would prove this to be true as the heavy darkness of heartbreak transformed into the thick cocoon of my becoming. In this solitary refinement with Him, in the secret place, I was being woven and spun by God into an entirely new being. In His mercy, this cocoon would not become a coffin but a doorway to destiny. I emerged on the other side, renamed and remade. Unbound by gravity, I took flight on the winds of a new current. God opened my brand-new wings to soar on the current of all He had reimagined me to be.

If you find yourself in a similar place, I encourage you to hold on. When God Himself is with you, the wilderness becomes a womb, a womb where the secret of the secret place with God is to protect your becoming as you give yourself fully to the solitary process of spiritual metamorphosis.

The formational fire of the wilderness is a holy test, a test John the Baptist passed over a lifelong process. John the Baptist didn't simply visit the wilderness; he lived there. If we look through the lens of our culture, we might place his lifestyle in the category of a lifelong trial of suffering. After all, no one would voluntarily establish themselves in such a desolate place. We want convenience and ease. We want the company of friends and peers. We want provision and plenty.

But what if wilderness solitude and obscurity with God— free from distraction and noise—is where the gold of intimacy is mined with God? What if, in God's upside-down Kingdom, obscurity with God is actually the doorway to healthy dependence and deliverance from the idol of visibility?

Overcoming the Idol of Visibility

Visibility. This word isn't inherently evil. It's important for God's sons and daughters to become a city on a hill and light in a dark world (Matthew 5:14-16). We are infused with God's Spirit to become the salt of the earth, and God will often position us in visible places to reflect His glory and proclaim His truth. After all, we can't give God glory for the stories we don't tell. Psalm 107:2 reminds us of the importance of using our voices: "Let the redeemed of the LORD tell their story—those he redeemed from the hand of the foe." The problem isn't visibility itself. The dangers arise from both human and cultural drives. We have a sin nature, and we are also set in a culture that often prioritizes visibility at all costs. In our world of social media algorithms, podcasts, and platforms, danger can surface in our vulnerable human hearts.

There's an important message here for those of us in the West, where one of our greatest fears is invisibility and irrelevance. Henri Nouwen, who left his role at Harvard to work with people who were intellectually disabled, addressed this with biblical wisdom in saying, "The leaders of the future will be the ones who dare to claim their irrelevance in the contemporary world as a divine vocation that allows them to enter into a deep solidarity with the anguish underlying all the glitter of success and to bring the light of Jesus there."[3]

Nouwen's words are a welcome contrast to a culture bent on the pursuit of visible popularity and power. But how do we parse this out practically? If we are meant to be a city on a hill, how do we faithfully live into this invitation while protecting ourselves from the snares of the world, the enemy, and the flesh as it relates to becoming visible?

Seek Intimacy with God

John the Baptist was invited into the fullness of his call by God because he was a person of integrity before Him. John's public persona matched his private devotion. But today, in our circles, when the responsibility and privilege of visibility is granted without a personal priority for proximity to God, there is not only danger to our communities—there is danger on a soul level. Influence for God without intimacy with God has serious implications that we can observe throughout the biblical narrative. The records of 1 and 2 Kings alone are a continuous dichotomy between those granted power who did evil in the sight of the Lord and those who did right in the eyes of God. The chronicles of the kings and rulers of old remind us of a timeless truth that is still coursing through our lived reality today: Power without the fear of the Lord always and eventually leads to corruption. John the Baptist's wilderness reality may have been solitary and wild, but it was also wildly protective. Distance from God is the number one reason visibility in His name can evolve into a curse instead of a blessing when sin sits on the seat of the human heart.

Ground Yourself in the Fear of the Lord

When the spiritual, moral, emotional, physical, mental, and relational tensions of visibility are not properly contended with through a heart grounded in the fear of the Lord, there are dangerous implications. This was not a presenting problem for John the Baptist because he had a robust history of silence and solitude with God, a history that gave way to God as his greatest influence. His life was lived in the crucible of full dependence. As crowds gathered and he faced the temptations of visibility, he knew how to abide in God as a person. The God who gave him his daily bread, shielded him from the perils of the wilderness, and clothed him with provision was the same God present in divinely ordained moments where courage, boldness, and obedience were at play.

Psalm 19:9 says, "The fear of the LORD is clean, enduring forever; the rules of the LORD are true, and righteous altogether" (ESV). A proper reverence and awe of the personhood of God. A loyalty to God and His Word. A yielding to His Spirit above all and before all. *This* is the narrow way that keeps the human heart clean. This was John the Baptist's doorway to intimacy, and it is ours as well.

Even if we know these truths intellectually, nothing will test the human heart more than the test of visibility, because in this space we are confronted with the temptation to replace the fear of the Lord with the fear of man.

Fear of rejection.

Fear of failure.

Fear of isolation.

To be human is to forfeit immunity to the elements of a home-sick world. We cannot live insulated lives, but we can live within the protective refuge of relational intimacy with God, in which we may feel the effects of a post-Eden world but not be mastered by them. When the primary voice we are attuned to is God's, we will walk into rooms grounded in His approval. We will speak in step with the Spirit's leading, and we will steward our lives to align with His will and His ways. John the Baptist's wilderness journey models the spiritual benefits of a life in which the appetite for human praise is starved and a resolute preference for God's approval is nourished. The result of John the Baptist's lifestyle was a heart free from the fear of man:

> When [John] saw many of the Pharisees and Sadducees
> coming to where he was baptizing, he said to them: "You

brood of vipers! Who warned you to flee from the coming wrath? Produce fruit in keeping with repentance. And do not think you can say to yourselves, 'We have Abraham as our father.' I tell you that out of these stones God can raise up children for Abraham. The ax is already at the root of the trees, and every tree that does not produce good fruit will be cut down and thrown into the fire."

MATTHEW 3:7-10

John the Baptist was unafraid to confront the religious leaders with God's truth. A heart centered on the fear of the Lord is unhindered by the need to prove, the desire to be relevant, or the trappings of fear.

A quantity of quality time in the safe sanctum of the secret place is the soil this kind of spiritual growth is grown in. John the Baptist drew crowds. He had a missional call of supernatural importance, and yet his wilderness solitude with God grew a level of spiritual maturity in him that prevented him from being mastered by the adulation *or* rejection of men. A life of intentional obscurity with God prevents us from trading the easy yoke of groundedness in God for the bondage of human outcomes.

Aim to Do Our Father's Will, Not Grow a Following

Like John the Baptist's, Jesus' aim was not to grow a following. His only aim was to do His Father's will. He is one with the Father, and He operates at His pace and on His timeline. Though Jesus' rhythm of life was lived in community, Scripture tells us He frequently withdrew to quiet places to pray. Jesus chose to prioritize moments of obscurity with God. This, too, is our invitation.

On any given week, as I engage in my life as an artist, spiritual director, and shepherd, I will often fulfill commitments the world might view as important. Frequently I will do so without posting about them on social media or otherwise disclosing them in public. I cannot tell you how many times I have sung for the masses and not taken a photo for public consumption. During the release of my third record, I remember feeling an unusually strong urge to abstain from regularly posting photos of the tour. This was a complex conviction for me since I have often felt like every opportunity for me is an opportunity for every little brown girl hoping to make a difference in the world. But in response to what I believe was the Spirit's prompting, I performed in amazing places during that tour only to withhold them from my Instagram account. Did I feel the tension in this? At times, yes. But as my flesh is crucified more and more, I've grown in my discernment of the Spirit's voice. This protects the practice of obscurity from becoming a legalistic requirement for holiness and keeps it more of a relational response to the real-time prompting of the Spirit.

Obscurity is a choice. A choice to be sensitive to the Spirit's leading. A choice to know when our urges are feeding the invisible monster of a desire for man's approval. It is a discipline that has spiritual benefits on a soul level. Here's the question we must ask when we wrestle with the tension of obscurity in a visible world: *Do I believe my friendship with God—my belief in His Word, my intimate prayer life with Him, and my yielding to the Spirit—has the final authority over my future? Or do I believe adhering to the world's systems of gain, which include incessant visibility, are necessary for me to enter the God-given fullness I was created for?*

Discerning the Prompting of God in Your Life

One of the greatest treasures John the Baptist's life holds for us in this cultural moment is the reality that he did not send himself on mission. He was sent by God. We live in a culture where this has become a critical question. Do we step into opportunities because we have been prompted by God . . . or are we sending ourselves? There are repercussions for a life led by self-determination in contrast to a life lived sent by the Spirit. Do we have the humility to ask, *Where is God moving?* and *How can I catch the wind of His activity to join Him where He is working?* We learn to discern and know God's voice in this through private, hidden devotion to Him. John the Baptist was sent on the winds of God's Spirit and nothing less. There is much meaning to be mined from this truth.

We Are Sent by God, Not Ourselves

John the Baptist did not nominate himself to prepare the way of the Lord. He was chosen. We read in Luke 3:2, "During the high-priesthood of Annas and Caiaphas, the word of God came to John son of Zechariah in the wilderness." John the Baptist first received a word from the Lord; *then* he was sent on mission with God.

In our modern-day, real-life context, waiting for prompting from the Lord has everything to do with our ability to pray and discern God's voice. In a noisy, distracted, success-oriented culture, this involves cultivating spaces for silence and solitude. In silence and solitude, our activity in God's name is primed to flow from the activity of God stirring in us. The soil of our life with God is the birthplace of true mission and calling. John the Baptist did not create a mission statement for his life or aim to capture the culture's gaze. He caught the current of God's activity, a force that had been supernaturally stirring since at least the time of the prophet Isaiah (Isaiah 40:3-5). These truths offer us wisdom in this hour. Decisions made in response to God's activity within us and around us are decisions that help us remain tethered to God Himself—and *un*tethered to the world and its outcomes.

We Are Sustained by God's Sufficiency, Not Our Own

What is born of God's Spirit will be sustained by His sufficiency. When something is born of the flesh, out of human urges that flow from the pride of life, it must be sustained by the flesh and will ultimately fail or fade. God's sovereign authority set John the Baptist's call in motion through Isaiah's prophetic foretelling, the angel's announcement, the Holy Spirit's infilling, and God's presence throughout his wilderness life. John was sustained by God's power, not his own. We are effective because of God's power, not our own.

The crowds gathered around John the Baptist not because of his charisma, cleverness, education, appearance, or any other human qualifications. He was effective simply because he was chosen by, sent from, and yielded to God. Crowds left the city to see him in the wilderness. Surely they were drawn to the sound of God breaking the silence of generations of darkness. They had a sense that John the Baptist was supernaturally appointed. This was due no doubt to the fact that he aimed the crowds upward to God and prepared them for Jesus. Being sent by God is an entrustment from Him. What we do with this entrustment determines everything. Whom we point people to when God sends them our direction is the difference between building our own finite, temporal kingdoms and building the everlasting Kingdom of God.

John the Baptist's life reminds us that obscurity with God centers us in the discipline of hearing and knowing His voice and guards us against the cultural dangers of visibility. As we look to John's life, we see some spiritually protective benefits of this practice that counter the soul-level threats posed to us in our own time and place.

- *Identity*: Obscurity with God prevents us from placing our identity in what we do (instead of in whom we know). Psalm 139 reminds us that we were fearfully and wonderfully made by God before we could do anything to earn His love. Obscurity guards us from falling prey to a rhythm of life focused on exterior achievements, upward mobility, or earthly fame at the expense of soul-level centeredness in God.

- *Loyalty*: Obscurity with God nourishes and protects the root system of our lives. We sustain relational intimacy with Him so that our hearts remain grounded in loyalty to Him above all else.

- *Humility*: Obscurity with God breeds humility. As we connect with His heart and His values, we are protected from self-reliance and strengthened in the foundation of Hebrews 11:6, which tells us that "without faith it is impossible to please God." We live our lives out of the belief that God rewards those who diligently seek Him in the secret place.

For some of us, in this life, obedience is its own reward. Such was the case for John the Baptist, a man fully yielded to God and therefore fully approved by Him. As pastor and author Alistair Begg says, "There is no ideal place to serve God except the place in which He sets you down."[4] No one proves this more than John the Baptist, whose radical loyalty to God teaches us something of what it means to walk in the submission of being sent, the certainty of God's conclusive authority, and the discipline of burying our life like a seed in private devotion. As we go into the world to prepare the way of the Lord for such a time as this, may we be drawn to the ancient way of wilderness obscurity, led by the Spirit out of man's line of sight and into the power of a hidden life of prayer in the sanctum of our secret place with God.

Reflection Questions

1. John the Baptist lived a life of radical loyalty to God. Have you ever felt appointed by God for a mission? How did you know you were being sent by God in a specific direction?

2. What are the primary invitations available to us in wilderness seasons?

3. How would you define the secret place? What does this practice of intimacy look like between you and God?

4. Visibility can often be the result of God's calling. When it comes, how can we protect ourselves from its snares?

FAILING FORWARD

Fully Formed through Disappointment

We live in a world where irrevocable dismissal can happen to anyone, anywhere and at any time. Cancel culture is the public rejection of someone who is either a perceived or a confirmed transgressor. The stakes are high in a culture where mass public outcry can make or break people, platforms, and missional movements. When we were children, our parents warned us not to place our hands near the hot surface of the kitchen stove. But if we dared to touch the scalding heat of that surface, blisters would form to prove it. We experienced pain and were left with marks to remind us of a bad decision that had led to bad consequences. Failure is life's great teacher because, once again, pain is the great motivator.

When we skinned our knees after our first bicycle ride without training wheels, we decided we would do anything to avoid another unwelcome encounter with the pavement. We steadied our legs and hands and pushed off for the next bike ride with more care and caution than before. When you've experienced the pain of failure, wisdom entails avoiding it again at all costs. We learn this from a young age. We store these lived experiences in the memory bank of who we are and vow to keep our distance from the dangers of a homesick world. We read books. We attend seminars. We accumulate data. We look to a world of progress and information as the primary source for transformation. But if a fully formed life of faith came down to successful cerebral processing, wouldn't we be good by now? If information were transformation, wouldn't all our problems be solved already?

It is unwise to think that here, millennia later, our technological advancements, higher education, societal progress, or increased knowledge of the world and its workings would stand a chance of relieving us, on a soul level, from the same spectrum of human weakness the fathers and the mothers of our faith faced. Information alone is not transformation, and information alone does not protect us from moral or spiritual collapse. Failure has a spiritual root system, a root system warring with the enemy of our souls, our own human bodies, and the perils of a homesick world. As such, failure can only be properly addressed when we acknowledge our own human frailty and our distinct need for God Himself—and when we tend to the root systems of our lives that need repair.

The life of Peter reminds us of these truths and that no one is immune to the realities of the human condition, not even someone who lived and communed with God incarnate Himself. In John 1:42 we read about how Jesus took a walk by the Sea of Galilee and called a lowly fisherman named Simon to Himself, giving him a new name: Peter. Peter's name means "rock," and this moment with Jesus would usher him into a divine journey of befriending Emmanuel—God with us—in a way that would fully form him into the rock Jesus would build His church upon. Scripture illustrates the winding road of Peter's becoming as his faith increased through exposure to Jesus as the true Messiah and son of God . . .

including before his relational collapse. Why is this important? Because this gives us a window into the development of his spiritual root system, a root system that would be thoroughly tested and tried through Peter's failure and throughout his life and ministry.

The Root Systems of Our Lives

Why is it important to talk about the root systems of our lives, and what are they? Root systems carry the power of invisible force and grow subterranean motivations that eventually break beyond the surface and into visible action. They are responsible for why we do what we do. Root systems originate in the soil of the stories we've lived to influence the way we see the world. When these root systems are flourishing, they are influenced primarily by our interaction with God's Word, His Spirit, and a story engaged in healing work with God and healthy community. Our internal root systems are singularly unique since none of us possess the same set of variables as anyone else. And yet there is enough universality in the human experience to provide a solid grid for us to explore this in more detail. We are so different, yet very much the same, by God's design, at our core. Dallas Willard describes the core dynamics of the human experience, or the soil of our lives, if you will, in six basic areas:

1. thought (images, concepts, judgments, inferences)
2. feeling (sensations, emotions)
3. choice (will, decisions, character)
4. body (actions, interactions with the physical world)
5. social context (personal and structural relations to others)
6. soul (the factor that integrates all the other aspects to form one life)[1]

Each of these layers comprises the soil our root systems will grow in and are interconnected in their importance in the framework of our own spiritual formation.

Spiritual formation in the life of a Christ follower is the process in which we are being formed into the likeness of Jesus and in which we are invited to cultivate the ground of our relationship with God so our intimacy with Him becomes *the* central root system from which all things grow. In a world obsessed with visible growth, it is vital to remember that in the divine order of life and living, everything we see begins deep beneath the surface. A seed is buried in the dark, watered by rain, and nourished by sunlight. It begins to germinate and grows a root system in the silence and secrecy of the invisible realm, layers and layers beneath what the human eye can detect.

Matthew 7:18 reminds us, "A good tree cannot bear bad fruit, and a bad tree cannot bear good fruit." The health of a tree is tethered to the health of its roots. This is an important metaphor for us as we consider Peter's three major pre-collapse encounters, and this is an important metaphor for our own spiritual formation.

It is our internal root systems that will sustain the burgeoning new life God wants to author under a protective layer of soil. When life's harsh winds, violent storms, hard freezes, and unexpected inclement weather occur, a healthy root system planted at the proper depth will remain intact and yield beauty from season to season. Visible growth is quite literally sustained through layers of invisible care.

Emphasis on the invisible can be a hard teaching in a culture where seeing is believing. But highlight reels and Hollywood buzz feeds do little to nourish us. Our culture emphasizes the topsoil of the exterior, but in the landscape of this age, if we're not intentional about planting and maintaining proper root systems, seeds of faith and devotion can easily fall on shallow ground and never take deep root. The good fruit on the good tree of your life and mine begins with what lies beneath the surface.

Peter's proximity to Jesus had been nourishing his relational root system with God for years. In much the same way, our proximity to God serves as a protective layer against the perils of our own humanity, the enemy's tactics, and the temptations of the world.

Peter's relational collapse after three years of close, intimate, real-time discipleship with Jesus came as a surprise to him, but it didn't surprise God, because He has always been faced with our human complexity. From Eve's error in Eden to the idolatry of the golden calf to the moments in view throughout this chapter, the spiritual formation of the mothers and fathers of our faith occurred in the complexity of their own failures and less-than-ideal circumstances. Formation happens in the mess. This is where God has always found us. We have all left the Garden. We have all wrestled with lies and loyalty as we've stood in the shadows of our own metaphorical trees of life. And yet some of our most spiritually formative moments have the potential to occur through failure and the opportunity to learn, unlearn, and relearn what is true.

Every day you and I breathe the air of a post-Eden world. We awake in a reality that is far from the harmony and perfection we were created from and for, but most of the time we live with a peripheral awareness of this reality. Sure, when I hit all the red lights on my way to a meeting or the grocery store is out of ripe avocados, I'm reminded that life doesn't work the way it's supposed to, but these mundane disappointments pale in comparison to what happens in the recesses of our hearts, minds, and bodies when a major loss or heartache unfolds.

Peter could not have been given a more solid foundation to stand on. He had been chosen by Jesus Himself and developed a close friendship with Him over a three-year period. He had witnessed the supernatural activity of God through His life and ministry firsthand, beginning with his election, when Peter had cast his net out for it to be miraculously filled with fish. A plethora of miracles had followed, including watching Jesus cast out demons, heal the sick, and feed the five thousand. But it wasn't what Jesus had done for others but Peter's personal encounters with Jesus Himself that provide more detail about the trajectory of his personal faith.

Notably, before his relational collapse, Peter had three formative experiences that give us rich insight into the development of the root systems of our faith and the soil of our interior life with God:

1. walking on water,
2. confessing Jesus as the Christ, and
3. witnessing the Transfiguration.

Peter Walks on Water

In Matthew 14 Peter finds himself being called out to meet Jesus on the waves of a stormy sea. Scripture tells us,

> Peter got out of the boat and walked on the water and
> came to Jesus. But when he saw the wind, he was afraid,
> and beginning to sink he cried out, "Lord, save me." Jesus
> immediately reached out his hand and took hold of him,
> saying to him, "O you of little faith, why did you doubt?"
> And when they got into the boat, the wind ceased.
> MATTHEW 14:29-32, ESV

Here we see Peter's humanity on display. His foundation cracked in a moment. The ground of his faith was split in two, not by the force of God's power but by the condition of his own heart. He may have been spending night and day with the Messiah Himself, witnessing countless divine acts, but these divine, wondrous acts did not keep him from being prone to wander, as is true for every hue and shade of the human heart along the spectrum of humanity. This hearkens back to the miracles of the Old Testament and what was revealed of human fragility then. Not even the plagues of Egypt, the miraculous deliverance from Pharaoh, and the supernatural wideness of a parted Red Sea were enough to prevent God's people from the idolatry of the golden calf.

This moment in Scripture reminds us that root systems nourished by reverence for the hand of God without proper reverence for and connection to God Himself as a person do not last. Miracles certainly have their place, but they are never meant to replace the relational foundation of trust in and intimacy with God as a friend in the sanctum of prayer.

Peter Confesses Jesus as the Christ

Despite Peter's crashing doubt on the treacherous waves of the sea, Matthew 16 reveals a much more convinced heart. The very moment of doubt that Peter's flesh, the enemy, and the world had contributed to for his destruction, God had undoubtedly used for his development:

> When Jesus came into the district of Caesarea Philippi, he asked his disciples, "Who do people say that the Son of Man is?" And they said, "Some say John the Baptist, others say Elijah, and others Jeremiah or one of the prophets." He said to them, "But who do you say that I am?" Simon Peter replied, "You are the Christ, the Son of the living God." And Jesus answered him, "Blessed are you, Simon Bar-Jonah! For flesh and blood has not revealed this to you, but

my Father who is in heaven. And I tell you, you are Peter, and on this rock I will build my church, and the gates of hell shall not prevail against it. I will give you the keys of the kingdom of heaven, and whatever you bind on earth shall be bound in heaven, and whatever you loose on earth shall be loosed in heaven."

MATTHEW 16:13-19, ESV

If you have ever thought, even for one second, that your doubts have cancelled your faith or God's commitment to finish what He started in you, I pray the power of this moment washes over you. God never gives up on His kids. In the words of Psalm 103:14 (NLT), "He knows how weak we are; he remembers we are only dust." Peter's faith was remade in a moment as the Holy Spirit Himself revealed Christ's identity to him. If this wasn't enough, Jesus also foreshadowed the role Peter would play in God's Kingdom come. But in the flurry of this divine revelation from the Spirit, let us not miss Jesus' authoritative announcement of what would rage against Peter's divine destiny. When He said, "The gates of hell shall not prevail against it," we know that Jesus was already present to Peter's future in the same way He is present to our own. Failure had not cancelled out the possibility of destiny; the harsh winds and violent storms would strengthen Peter's root systems. Here we see that not even the mess of Peter's complexity—or the mess of our own—would cancel out God's personal and present love, His divine call, or the continuous edification of His church.

Peter Witnesses the Transfiguration

Six days later Jesus took with him Peter, James, and John the brother of James, and led them privately up a high

mountain. And he was transfigured before them. His
face shone like the sun, and his clothes became white as
light. Then Moses and Elijah also appeared before them,
talking with him. So Peter said to Jesus, "Lord, it is good
for us to be here. If you want, I will make three shelters—
one for you, one for Moses, and one for Elijah." While he
was still speaking, a bright cloud overshadowed them, and
a voice from the cloud said, "This is my one dear Son,
in whom I take great delight. Listen to him!" When the
disciples heard this, they were overwhelmed with fear and
threw themselves down with their faces to the ground.
But Jesus came and touched them. "Get up," he said. "Do
not be afraid." When they looked up, all they saw was
Jesus alone.

MATTHEW 17:1-8, NET

As if it hadn't been enough for Peter to momentarily defy the
laws of physics by walking on water and to receive divine revelation
from the third person of the Trinity, who had revealed Christ's identity to him, now Peter had seen Jesus supernaturally transfigured.
This was holy ground where Moses and Elijah also appeared and
the voice of God proclaimed who Jesus is. In all time and space
there is perhaps no greater evidence Peter or you and I could ask
for than this level of divine confirmation. The natural world and
the divine converged in a holy confluence of glory, white light,
and the appearance of fathers of the faith gone before us, accompanied by the voice of God Almighty and a bright cloud. I invite
you to consider the lengths to which God has revealed Himself
through wonder and power. No one present could dare question
the validity of this moment. If failure could be avoided by accumulation of supernatural confirmation, experiential legitimacy,

and relational equity, Peter's faith would have been 100 percent bulletproof. But the one variable these strong defenses could not cancel out is the complex vulnerability of the human heart.

Peter's Relational Collapse

If healthy spiritual formation is cultivated in the root systems of our lives, the enemy, the flesh, and the world fertilize the weeds that choke out this growth. If spiritual maturity blooms from layers of invisible care that begin and end in the sanctum of our life with God, nothing will test the health of these layers like disappointment, trouble, and loss. Peter faced the growing tension of these threats with mounting intensity as he approached his relational collapse. His life with Jesus had never been a life of ease, but as the disciples approached the time of Christ's crucifixion, their human hearts began to wrestle with the impending loss of the One who had called and appointed them by name. The One they had broken bread with. The One who had looked them in the eyes so personally and given them the gift of being believed in. The One they had pledged their entire lives to follow. Imagine living with and befriending the Great Shepherd for years. Following his every move and every word . . . and then being confronted with the reality that life as they knew it, with Him, would end. They would have to follow Him to His own death and then experience the death of life as they once knew it.

In the Gospel of Matthew, we see that Jesus predicted Peter's denial:

Jesus told them, "This very night you will all fall away on account of me, for it is written:

"'I will strike the shepherd,
     and the sheep of the flock will be scattered.'

But after I have risen, I will go ahead of you into Galilee."

Peter replied, "Even if all fall away on account of you,
I never will."

"Truly I tell you," Jesus answered, "this very night,
before the rooster crows, you will disown me three
times."

But Peter declared, "Even if I have to die with you,
I will never disown you."

MATTHEW 26:31-35

Later in the chapter, we see Jesus' prediction come to pass:

Peter was sitting out in the courtyard, and a servant
girl came to him. "You also were with Jesus of Galilee,"
she said.

But he denied it before them all. "I don't know what
you're talking about," he said.

Then he went out to the gateway, where another
servant girl saw him and said to the people there, "This
fellow was with Jesus of Nazareth."

He denied it again, with an oath: "I don't know
the man!"

After a little while, those standing there went up to
Peter and said, "Surely you are one of them; your accent
gives you away."

Then he began to call down curses, and he swore to
them, "I don't know the man!"

Immediately a rooster crowed. Then Peter remembered the word Jesus had spoken: "Before the rooster crows, you will disown me three times." And he went outside and wept bitterly.

MATTHEW 26:69-75

Mine the Meaning

Therapist and professor Dan Allender speaks to the inevitability of human failure when he states: "To experience brokenness and humiliation, all you have to do is lead."[2] Peter had been surrounded by scrutiny as a follower of Jesus and was undoubtedly in a markedly visible position. But if we're honest with ourselves, we will identify with his human fragility, whether we are in formal leadership or not. Here we see the fury of a storm test the strength of the root system of Peter's faith, a root system wholly nourished by three years of supernaturally charged, face-to-face discipleship with Jesus. What can we learn from Peter about the role of root systems in our own spiritual formation?

1. *Proximity to God is protective and grounding but does not make us immune to the reality of our own human weaknesses.* On this side of heaven, we would be wise to walk in the fear of the Lord and in a profound sobriety of what we are capable of when in the wrong place at the wrong time.

2. *The deeper and healthier our relational root system is (with God, in Word and Spirit), the stronger the storms it can withstand when the winds of our own weaknesses threaten the stability of our faith.* When we abide in God, we cultivate a life of inner confidence, in which the force of God's activity in

us stands as a strong confirmation against the fury of life's questions and complexities.

3. *Pain and suffering are revelatory.* They reveal the true condition of our hearts, the reality of our humanity, and the depth of our character. The strength of our rootedness in God is exposed in times like these. These moments help us identify our vulnerabilities so we can partner with God to contend for healing and freedom in those areas to prevent repetition of harmful cycles.

Mine the Purpose

What the enemy intends for our devastation, God intends for our development. We see this throughout the biblical narrative. God does not avoid the failures of His people but instead transforms every ending into a new beginning.

Moses lands in the back side of the desert only to encounter the living God in a burning bush and to receive a call that leads him into destiny.

Joseph is displaced and traumatized by his brothers only to be vindicated by God and to save them and the people of Israel in the end.

Peter fails multiple times as the words Jesus spoke over him materialize, but the root system of his faith will ultimately hold strong, and he will go on to live into the name Christ gave him. Peter indeed becomes the rock on which Jesus builds His church, and in the mercy of God, not even his own failures alter his destiny.

If you've lived some life, maybe you identify with Peter. I do because in part I've never wanted others' words spoken over me to become self-fulfilling prophecy. His story resonates with me because historically I, too, have struggled with a leaning toward self-sufficiency and a denial of my own human limitations.

The Lie of Self-Sufficiency

Early on in life my approach to my own complexity in this area was to do more and try harder, in my own strength, to make sure the negative sentences others spoke over me never came to pass. This posture of striving began when I inherited underdog status by being raised in a marginalized community. It only intensified when I entered the music industry. I could feel the tension of the cultural narrative nipping at my heels in what I felt sure was the sunset of my youth. I was thirty-five, and I could see forty lining the last horizon of possibility as I knew it. I felt the looming dread that accompanied the standard cultural script: *If you don't succeed by twenty-nine, you're not going to succeed.*

While I never subscribed to others' version of success, I longed to steward my calling well. I was several years past twenty-nine, but few words triggered me on a neurobiological level more than "You're not going to succeed." I had already been told by music industry executives and professional songwriters that Hispanic women don't stand much chance in the Christian music industry. But I knew my calling was from God Himself, and I knew it wasn't going to simply disappear into thin air even if it didn't align with music-industry norms. My call would forever echo off the walls of my heart if it did not find a way out of my body. And if it had nowhere to go, the call would become a longing, and the longing would become an ache. I had learned to live in the tension of the God dream that had been placed in me and the world I had been born into with the "wrong" pedigree and a less-than-likely set of variables. Even though I had learned the art of a good Amy Winehouse–esque winged eyeliner and had a high level of aesthetic appreciation, I was honest with myself when I looked in the mirror. I was a long way from Miss America. The music industry had a template for artists, and I didn't fit it.

But as I saw it, I had no choice. I had to steward my calling. Allowing others' words to disqualify me was not an option. In 2015 I set out to make my third record at a definite crossroads in life. It was an important record because for the very first time I conjured up the gumption to enter the creative process with determination, vigilance, and a visceral hunger to push back on the limits, ceilings, and assumptions that had been spoken over me, time after time, as a woman in the music industry. "We don't need you to weigh in on this part of the creative process." "You can't really be part of this aspect of the song." "We're going to call in someone else to play that piano part you wrote"—words I never expected to hear as a proficient keys player of twenty years!

Perhaps like Peter, I had something to prove. I felt I had to prove the executives wrong. This was the first mistake I made, a weed in my internal root system that was very much storied for me. Entering any endeavor with an air of striving and hunger for man's approval is a recipe for frustration at best and disaster at worst.

So I set my face like a flint to the north, and I recorded, engineered, comped, and tuned my own vocals in my own studio until the wee hours of the morning with my husband, my four-year-old, and my eight-year-old close by. I did my own preproduction, from programming drums to fine-tuning MIDI keys. I tweaked parts until they were absolute perfection in my mind and swam in an ocean of musical minutiae, sometimes until 4:00 a.m. Then

I would rise and shine at 6:45 a.m. to get kids off to school and work a full day at the studio with only a short lunch break. It was intense. But I knew no one would care more about these songs and this work than I did, and I didn't expect them to. I worked twenty- to twenty-two-hour days during the making of this record in what felt like an endless gestational period. But the desire in me to prove the industry wrong was the fire no one could save me from stoking.

At the end of what I referred to then as a "labor-intensive sowing season," I will never forget how God brought harvest from scattered seeds. It became my most critically acclaimed record at the time. I booked a successful tour and recouped my money within two months of said tour, but I was falling apart. My physical, mental, emotional, and relational health had been sacrificed on the altar of this success, and the carnage was widespread and undeniable. I will never forget standing at the edge of the Santa Monica Mountains for a tour photo shoot. I was surrounded by beauty in the wonder of California, and the smell of the Pacific Ocean filled the air on a perfect, sixty-five-degree day, but I was a shell of a person and withering away. I had stopped eating, and sleep was at a minimum. I was on a mission to save the world, but at the age of thirty-six, I was the one who needed saving.

Let me tell you something. All the success in the world doesn't mean much when you are laying your very body, mind, and soul on the altar of achievement to secure it. The idol of man's approval had granted me momentary public success, but the private fallout was disastrous. I was suffering from the worst case of burnout possible. My marriage, my body, my mind, and my soul were barely surviving. I finished the last tour date in May of the following year and then determined to settle into a local church. I needed a full stop. I needed to sleep. I needed to eat. I needed to heal. I needed to mine the meaning of how I had let myself get to this breaking point.

I began to ask good questions, questions I now ask in the wake of any failure or rupture that needs repair:

- *What am I discerning from God amid all this?*
- *Is this experience part of a pattern I have observed in my life?*
- *Is there a root system in my life that needs repair?*

A mentor of mine once told me that no one benefits from a lie. The place where that happens the most is deep down inside our very own hearts. Sometimes we see what we want to see. Sometimes we see what we have the capacity to see. Many of us know many things in our gut but have been conditioned to dismiss those instincts. Yet it is the truth that sets us free. And friends, it's time to move forward in truth. Sometimes this is relevant in our relationships with others, and sometimes this is relevant to our relationships with God and ourselves.

How do I know this? Failure. I had lied to myself. For a short time it was convenient to tell myself everything was okay, but as I sat in the ashes of my own undoing, it was time to finally be honest and confront the truth. When I carved out the space to mine the meaning of this season of my life with these questions, the answers began to wash my soul with an amount of clarity I had not had for years. It's the truth that sets us free—if we have the courage to face it.

Artist Jason Upton once said, "Jesus doesn't avoid pain—he transforms it."[3] The process of transformation can commence only once we've allowed the truth to set us free from lies and avoidance. These archenemies of spiritual formation block the doorway to truth.

In hindsight, I fought hard to reach the fullness of my potential, and while there were some benefits to the development of my skill set and to the overall project, I also learned that if we're not careful, workaholism can become a little-*g* god that can bind us to a mindset of striving. This mindset can deplete us spiritually, mentally, physically, emotionally, and relationally while enslaving us to a life rooted in the idolatry of achievement, self-sufficiency, and the approval of man.

I learned that succumbing to perfectionism is not the same as offering excellence. Excellence is simply about receiving what God gives us and responding to Him with faithful stewardship. Excellence is about working with a proper fear of the Lord, an awe and amazement of Him. Perfectionism is the chronic displeasure of everything we deem less than superior. It was bondage, rooted not in the fear of the Lord but in the fear of man and a desire to people please. I learned that working from God's pleasure within us is vastly different from working *for* God's pleasure. I learned that God was already pleased with me through Jesus, His Son, and my attempts at earning anything more than what He had already given was a false gospel rooted in transactionalism. Failure was the great teacher because pain was the great motivator that led me to ask transformational questions and to have the courage to answer those questions with nothing less than the truth.

I discovered that when you reach your own professed "Promised Land" the wrong way, the milk and honey don't taste so sweet. What my heart truly craved was not in the liner notes of a critically acclaimed album. My heart longed for an intimate friendship with God the Father, the Son, and the Holy Spirit. My heart wanted to shepherd people into a deeper relationship with Him. All my striving would never set this in motion. All the things I was trying to force could never produce these results because the things I truly longed for were *unforced* gifts. The antidote wasn't in a passionate approach of doing more or trying harder. The answer would come in a metamorphosis of motive. Surrender and obedience first, then passion, then endurance with a respectful sobriety of my weak points and tendencies.

All this, the fruit of failure. Beauty from the ashes of extreme burnout.

Much like with Peter, God remade me in the fires of my own collapse. Transformation began with new practices. I never stopped working hard to steward my call, but I began to take the Sabbath, a twenty-four-hour period of rest and delight, very seriously. In author Pete Scazzero's book *Emotionally Healthy Spirituality*, he says, "The essence of being in God's image is our ability, like God, to stop. We imitate God by stopping our work and resting. If we can stop for one day a week, or for mini-Sabbaths each day (the Daily Office), we touch something deep within us as image bearers of God. Our human brain, our bodies, our spirits, and our emotions become wired by God for the rhythm of work and rest in him."[4]

I began to see the Sabbath as an act of trusting God with all the people, things, dreams, and projects I couldn't control. Contemplative prayer followed. Sleep. Rest. Margin. Wonder. These all became new spiritual practices that yielded life, inspiration, renewal, joy, and a closer awareness of God's activity and the Spirit's leading and movement. I stopped doing more and trying harder and began every day with a desire to notice the activity of God in and around me and to simply receive what was being given through the gift of knowing God as a person.

Failure is frequently an opportunity to become more fully formed. Our willingness to mine the meaning of it all with God and safe people helps us move forward, free and into deeper intimacy with the One who has always been in the work of rebuilding the ruins of our lives.

God's love lives in the tension of the now and the not yet. Jesus knew Peter would be sifted, but He still loved Peter and had a divine call on his life. He knew Peter's potential, and Jesus was committed to finishing the work He had started in Peter when He had first called him as a washed-up fisherman on the shores of the Sea of Galilee.

Failure offers many gifts. One of them is the authority to speak truth mined from lessons learned. Transformation turns to gold when wounds become wisdom. Peter would go on to walk in the authority of a restored life, preaching the gospel and even raising the dead (Acts 9:40). The rises and falls of his faith journey encourage us to remember that no season is final where the transformational power of God is at play. But miracles were not the only marker of Peter's supernatural restoration. Through fire and flood God had built the kind of character and godliness into Peter that would result in these final words. As Peter prepared his friends for his passing, he left them with evidence that his heart had been fully formed from the inside out. His witness went deep beneath the surface and grew from time-tested root systems that yielded the fruit of obedience to the end.

> His divine power has given us everything we need for a
> godly life through our knowledge of him who called us by
> his own glory and goodness. Through these he has given
> us his very great and precious promises, so that through
> them you may participate in the divine nature, having
> escaped the corruption in the world caused by evil desires.
> For this very reason, make every effort to add to
> your faith goodness; and to goodness, knowledge;

and to knowledge, self-control; and to self-control, perseverance; and to perseverance, godliness; and to godliness, mutual affection; and to mutual affection, love. For if you possess these qualities in increasing measure, they will keep you from being ineffective and unproductive in your knowledge of our Lord Jesus Christ. But whoever does not have them is nearsighted and blind, forgetting that they have been cleansed from their past sins.

Therefore, my brothers and sisters, make every effort to confirm your calling and election. For if you do these things, you will never stumble, and you will receive a rich welcome into the eternal kingdom of our Lord and Savior Jesus Christ.

2 PETER 1:3-11

That last line reminds us, once again, that we have a soul set on an eternal trajectory, a trajectory that even failure does not have the final word on when we choose to aim our hearts upward in loyalty to God above all else. God does not cosign on cancel culture, because where the resurrection power of the Cross is concerned, "Jesus doesn't avoid pain—he transforms it."

Reflection Questions

1. Peter's proximity to Jesus was developmental to his spiritual formation and yet did not make him immune to the perils of his own humanity. What can we learn from this?

2. How is failure an opportunity to become more fully formed?

3. Disappointment and loss can be revelatory. What do you think is at the heart of someone who revolts when confronted with disappointment?

4. As you reflect on your own failures, have you invited God into those places to help you mine the meaning so the wounds can be transformed into wisdom?

THE TOMB IS A WOMB

Becoming People of Rebirth

Have you ever experienced a season in which a particular message kept resurfacing? A season in which a trail of unmistakable moments seemed to be leading you somewhere, each moment like a clue lighting the path to new insight or revelation? As time passes you begin to wonder whether it's your imagination or whether Someone greater is at work.

I once heard a wise man say, "Coincidences are God's way of getting our attention."[1] At times I refer to this as the activity of God. In these moments God is trying to bring something to bear in our stories, and He's interacting with the natural world to supernaturally open our hearts to receive a message that is critical for us to pray into and discern.

This was the case when one of my friends of fifteen years sent me a text. It read: "I was researching eagles this week. Did you know mother eagles encourage eaglets to leave the nest and take flight by placing sharp objects in the nest so the discomfort will prompt them to let go, catch the current, and learn to fly?"

She happened to send this to me when one of the brightest corners of my calling had grown in complexity. But I didn't want to believe God could be leading me to let go of a season I once loved—or the calling that had fueled it. So I didn't leave the nest. Then one day I was hiking with my son at Radnor Lake State Park, a Nashville nature preserve full of wildlife and wonder. We were finishing up when I felt a nudge to stop and listen to a man with a professional camera talking to a few people. As I walked closer, I overheard, "Did you know when mother eagles prepare to release their young into the wild they bring sharp objects to the nest? Once covered by the comfort of feathers, these sharp objects are strategically placed where the eaglets will become so uncomfortable, they'll have no choice but to fly."

By this point I knew God was orchestrating these unexpected patterns—yet we can *know* God is speaking and still brush up against the tension of our own internal resistance. But in God's kindness, a third prompting came through a time of fasting. In silence and solitude I began to feel God's gentle nudge shepherd my heart with the message *It's time to let go.* God's patient pursuit of me had culminated in a very clear directive. *I'm asking you to leave the nest.*

Ecclesiastes 3 tells us there is a season for every activity under the heavens. Change is inevitable. This means God will always be our one and only permanent home, in this life and in the life to come. But in my journey, more times than not, I have failed to catch the current of God's will because I resist change. I can become too attached to comfort, too fearful to fly. Only when the nest becomes uncomfortable do I typically begin to question the plan. Sometimes we have to experience the pain of overstaying in a season to discern it's time to move on . . . to surrender.

Pain causes us to pray and ask what God may be trying to bring to bear through the unresolved tension that surfaces in any given season and circumstance. In God's line of sight these uncomfortable eagle-nest promptings were a gentle way to invite me into a season's ending. He was asking me to let go of the idol of comfort and predictability to send me forward on the winds of a new tour that would give me the opportunity to further develop and even expand my gifting into new areas. I couldn't see it then but my yes to this tour would mark the death of my former self, begin a gestational period for the expansion of my calling, and lead to an entire rebirth as fear lost its grip on me and I was given new vision for the fullness of all God had designed me to become.

Here's what I'd like to submit to you: I did not control the timing, process, or outcome of any of these events. I simply discerned my way through them and stewarded what God wanted to impart. Transformation is cyclical and seasonal, and much like creation, we have little to say in how our world will turn on its axis. All we know is that this beautiful blue-and-green planet will remain tender to the touch of a God who is the master orchestrator of both visible and invisible.

This may feel like a hard teaching in a world that reveres formulaic certainty. But throughout this book and the stories within, we have witnessed one of the foundational realities of spiritual formation: We are not forming ourselves; we are being formed. Just as the seasons yield to God's activity, just as the whole world turns by the force of a love we cannot quite comprehend, we learn to yield. We learn to trust. Trust is the soul-level participation required for transformation. We bury our seeds of faith in the ground of our lives and then trust the great Gardener to send sun and rain. The same God who holds creation together can be trusted with the work of fully forming us to become good trees that bear the good fruit of Christlikeness. This process is personal and founded on the belief that God is the giver of every good and perfect gift (James 1:17) and our role is to simply receive what is being given. But what happens when the season we're given isn't the season we want or when the timing and/or the outcome is laced in mystery? This is exactly the tension we long to avoid . . . but exactly the formational fire the faith of our fathers and mothers was forged in.

As we live and breathe in a culture driven by results, we can forget these age-old truths and instead opt in to the lie that true transformation is just one good equation away. And if we are not sober-minded, our way of thinking about our own spiritual formation can slip into the category of self-help, where our surrendered prayers evolve into self-propelled goals. Goals that sit on the seat of lordship, where only God was meant to reign. We can subconsciously adopt a striving mentality, in which our hearts become tethered to outcomes more than to God Himself. But what if faith isn't about performance or a "do more, try harder" mentality? What if faith is simply about receiving what is being given from God's hand, in His way and on His timeline? What if faith is simply about yielding like the seasons?

If there's one truth that echoes throughout the entire biblical narrative and every chapter of this book, it is this: *We do not control the process of our own spiritual formation.* We yield to the One who does and participate through obedience.

We surrender to the sovereignty of a God who is not conceptual but personal. His love is the guiding force over all creation and over the landscape of our lives, cultivating the soil of our souls to grow us into the fullness of who He uniquely created us to be. A journey of faith rooted in relational communion with God is not a journey of doing more in our own strength. It is a path personally led by His hand through seasons of death, resurrection, and life. The apostle Paul's lifelong journey of faith illustrates this cycle beautifully and helps us understand what it means to yield to God, who ordains times and seasons to transformational ends.

Paul (also called Saul) of Tarsus was probably born between AD 1 and AD 5. A well-educated Pharisee, he became a zealous persecutor of Christians before he was led—by a force greater than his own will, intellect, or gifting—into a great transformation. From his face-to-face encounter with Jesus on the road to Damascus to his ardent evangelism and discipleship efforts later, Paul has become a beacon of hope for the magnitude of God's grace and power. We see this take place in three transformational seasons in Paul's life, all recorded in the biblical narrative. These three seasons produced three transformational expressions of God's love and have parallels to our own lives as well:

1. in death, God reimagines;
2. in resurrection, God re-creates; and
3. in life, God redeems.

In Death, God Reimagines

Paul's radical spiritual rebirth was initiated by an experience that marked the death of his former self. His encounter with Jesus on the road to Damascus was a divine interruption signifying the beginning of God's plan to reimagine the trajectory of his life, faith, and calling.

> Saul, still breathing threats and murder against the
> disciples of the Lord, went to the high priest and asked
> him for letters to the synagogues at Damascus, so that if
> he found any belonging to the Way, men or women, he
> might bring them bound to Jerusalem. Now as he went

on his way, he approached Damascus, and suddenly a
light from heaven shone around him. And falling to
the ground, he heard a voice saying to him, "Saul, Saul,
why are you persecuting me?" And he said, "Who are
you, Lord?" And he said, "I am Jesus, whom you are
persecuting. But rise and enter the city, and you will be
told what you are to do." The men who were traveling
with him stood speechless, hearing the voice but seeing
no one. Saul rose from the ground, and although his
eyes were opened, he saw nothing. So they led him by
the hand and brought him into Damascus. And for three
days he was without sight, and neither ate nor drank.

ACTS 9:1-9, ESV

This encounter Paul (here called Saul) had with the living
Christ ushered him into the doorway of transformation by way
of death to his former self, marked by loss and powerlessness.
Paul experienced both. He lost the core belief he had founded his
faith upon as a highly trained Jew educated by a respected rabbi
named Gamaliel (Acts 22:3). His entire upbringing and religious
worldview as one who persecuted Christ followers imploded in
one moment as he encountered the Messiah—Jesus, the Son of
God. The One Stephen had called out to when he was stoned in
Paul's presence is indeed alive, and Paul could not unsee Jesus.
His conceptual faith in God had become a living person, a person
whose power he could no longer dismiss or deny.

In seasons of death we are frequently presented with new
truths, truths our eyes were once blinded to. Once we see these
truths, we cannot *un*know them. In a spiritually transformational
season of death, loss and powerlessness do not destroy us. Instead,
in God's hands, they develop and shape us as they reveal new

insight. They propel us on the winds of change into forward movement where we catch the current of a new sobriety, the momentum of all that cannot be unseen, undone, or hidden. In the blink of an eye Paul was changed by a level of powerlessness unlike any before this moment. He not only lost the validity of his vision of faith in God as a religious Pharisee, he also temporarily lost physical sight. This is a metaphor for what the coming days and decades would bring to the doorstep of his own spiritual formation. The loss and powerlessness of this moment was but a foreshadowing of a Hebrews 11 kind of faith where, like Abraham, Paul would not know where he was going. His blindness primed him to surrender control. He would die to himself and to his former vision of a flourishing life. Paul would be led by the hand of the Great Shepherd. A hand he had only observed from afar, through the dimly lit glass of the Old Testament, would now be experienced in a flood of light as Emmanuel, God with us.

God does some of His best work in the crucible of seasons where life as we've known it is falling away. This reality echoes Jesus' words in Matthew 16:24-25:

> Jesus said to his disciples, "Whoever wants to be my disciple must deny themselves and take up their cross and follow me. For whoever wants to save their life will lose it, but whoever loses their life for me will find it."

In God's upside-down Kingdom, losing is finding and dying to self is the doorway to spiritual rebirth.

In the hands of a God who is in the work of reimagination, death's dark tomb becomes a womb, a secret place where something new begins to grow in a gestational period of trust. This brings us to our next phase in the cycle of transformation.

In Resurrection, God Re-Creates

A new seed is sown inside us and cultivated through a gestational period of mystery and trust in equal parts. In this space God is trying to bring something new to bear, but first it must be hidden and nurtured in the secret place with Him.

God turned the dark tomb of Paul's life into a womb where

- his faith in God was re-created through the miraculous and
- his zeal was re-created, transformed by God's Spirit into usefulness in God's Kingdom.

There was a disciple at Damascus named Ananias. The Lord said to him in a vision, "Ananias." And he said, "Here I am, Lord." And the Lord said to him, "Rise and go to the street called Straight, and at the house of Judas look for a man of Tarsus named Saul, for behold, he is praying, and he has seen in a vision a man named Ananias come in and lay his hands on him so that he might regain his sight." But Ananias answered, "Lord, I have heard from many about this man, how much evil he has done to your saints at Jerusalem. And here he has authority from the chief priests to bind all who call on your name." But the Lord said to him, "Go, for he is a chosen instrument of mine to carry my name before the Gentiles and kings and the children of Israel. For I will show him how much he must suffer for the sake of my name." So Ananias departed and entered the house. And laying his hands on him he said, "Brother Saul, the Lord Jesus who appeared to you on the road by which you came has sent me so that you may regain your sight and be filled with the Holy Spirit." And immediately something like scales fell from his eyes, and he regained his sight. Then he rose and was baptized; and taking food, he was strengthened.

ACTS 9:10-19, ESV

Paul's vision of faith was completely re-created by not only his encounter with Jesus but also the restoration of his physical sight. This miraculous undoing is transformational because God did something for Paul he could not do for himself. God supernaturally overshadowed the natural, and Paul was filled with the Holy Spirit, baptized, and strengthened by God for a coming re-creation. In re-creation the spiritual concept of reimagination begins to develop beyond internal experience and into external action. In the life of Paul, this re-creative activity of God would lead to a life of service that would alter the course of biblical history through the transformation of his calling. However, the series of events that crescendoed into this moment are a testament to the fact that transformation is spiritual at its core. God's guiding force of love saw the horizon of possibility beyond Paul's own limited wisdom and understanding and ordained a series of moments that would have a before-and-after effect on his life. This level of reimagination and re-creation was clearly not Paul's doing. He was not forming himself. He was being formed.

As Paul was filled with God's Spirit, the re-creative activity of God overflowed into the reformation of his inherent gifts and qualities. The zeal that once fueled his determination to persecute believers was redeemed into a holy resolve to proclaim the name of Jesus and champion the movement of the gospel.

For some days he was with the disciples at Damascus.
And immediately he proclaimed Jesus in the synagogues,
saying, "He is the Son of God." And all who heard him
were amazed and said, "Is not this the man who made
havoc in Jerusalem of those who called upon this name?
And has he not come here for this purpose, to bring them
bound before the chief priests?" But Saul increased all the
more in strength, and confounded the Jews who lived in
Damascus by proving that Jesus was the Christ.

ACTS 9:19-22, ESV

God gestationally grew Paul's faith so it could live in the light of
action. The reimagination of his identity led to the re-creation of
his calling. This leads us to our third season in Paul's transformation, the longest and most enduring season of all.

In Life, God Redeems

While Paul undoubtedly cycled through other seasons of death
and resurrection in certain areas of his life, as we all do, there is no
doubt that Paul's unlikeliness—as a Pharisee and persecutor turned
follower of Christ—had been transformed over a lifetime into intimacy with God that led to influence for God. The mercy of Jesus
found Saul of Tarsus in a light that blinded him only to give him a
second sight, a sight that could see God's Kingdom right.

In the words of theologian Frederick Buechner, "Even in
the midst of suffering there is a God who is with us and for us
and will never let us go."[2] It was a few miles outside the city of
Damascus that Paul made the same overwhelming discovery. He
was on his way to bring members of the heretical sect who called
themselves Christians to Jerusalem for punishment when Christ

himself appeared, called him by name, and gave him a new faith to live and die for, a faith that led him to write years later, "I am convinced that neither death, nor life . . . nor things that are present, nor things to come . . . nor anything else in creation will be able to separate us from the love of God in Christ Jesus our Lord" (Romans 8:38-39, NET).

And in what was a transformational act of God, God did what He does best. He overrode every disqualifying variable that could hinder Paul's acceptance into a newly redeemed life. A checkered past, human dismissal, and the persecution that lined the halls of Paul's history would not have the final say. The mercy of God that found Paul on the road to Damascus became the power of God that brought to bear new life.

God redeemed the story of a man who had once used his life and gifts to try to destroy the Kingdom to now build it. God once again chose the unlikely and made him likely through the power of His Spirit.

Along the way Paul's rebirth reflected a new confidence—not in formulas, systems of control, or religious pedigree, but in the transforming power of his Trinitarian God. And in the crucible of a lifetime of ministry in relationship with his Trinitarian God, Paul authored more books of the Bible than any other writer.[3] From witnessing the stoning of Stephen to preaching the gospel on missionary journeys that established over a dozen churches, Paul went from being led by the hand of God in blindness to being led by His hand into greatness. But this kind of greatness would not lead Paul to ascend to success as the world defines it. This kind of greatness would lead him, as it leads all of us who follow Christ, into the long, lowly descent of humility and service.

As Paul healed the sick, cast out demons, and raised the dead by the power of the Holy Spirit and in the name of the One he had once persecuted, he also suffered shipwrecks both literal and metaphorical. He endured hardship for the sake of the gospel, on a level many of us cannot begin to understand.

Ultimately Paul was martyred, which brings up an important point for us to consider: Paul's life of redemption was not absent of pain and mystery. This is important since here in the West our idealism can do violence to our ability to recognize and embrace seasons of redemption when they are less than perfect. Because God's goal for us is to become like Jesus and to nourish the seeds of our faith to become good trees that bear good fruit, every life season will have both sun and rain. Both are necessary to maintain healthy root systems, root systems that can withstand the furious winds of life.

Paul knew that he could not boast in anything or anyone but the power of Christ working in him (Galatians 6:14). He was aware of his unlikeliness just as much as he was aware of God's call. Yet Paul did not allow the world's standards to overshadow God's standards and committed his life to live faithfully into the fullness of all God had destined for him to become. His journey reminds us that in every season there is something new God is trying to bring to fruition if we will yield to His timing and His ways.

As Paul's rebirth reveals, the extent of our surrender to the times and seasons God ushers us into will directly impact the level of transformation God desires to bring to bear.

All creation yields to the loving intent of the One who made all things and holds all things together. Every season in nature is a reimagination of the last, and this is also true for the seasons of our lives. Autumn's final exhale is a surrender to winter's quiet clearing. Winter's decrescendo always and eventually turns into the glorious unfolding of spring. We meet God in transitional dependence as we yield to the seasons and times He has chosen to allow in His sovereign line of sight. We can be sure every ending and every tomb is a brand-new beginning . . . a womb in which God is stirring in the dark to bring new life to light.

Reflection Questions

1. God is the One who ordains times and seasons. Can you recall a time in your life when He was inviting you to trust Him with a season's end? How did you experience God's presence in that space?

2. Paul's encounter with Jesus on the road to Damascus was a divine interruption that led to a divine detour. How can we be more open to God's divine interruptions and more present to His activity in our lives? What obstacles keep you from having the availability to notice where God is moving?

3. Why was Paul's blindness an important development in his transition from Pharisee to follower of Christ?

4. Oftentimes the extent of our surrender will be the extent of our transformation. What is God asking you to surrender in this season?

5. What is significant about God's choice of Paul as one of the most prolific authors in the Bible, and how does this further prove that God chooses unlikely people to love and partner with?

THE RETURNING

Living in the Way of Jesus

I've always had a deep love for Jesus. I remember feeling the flutter of curiosity around who He is even as a child. Oneness with God clothed in our human skin holds layers upon layers of meaning, and I had layers upon layers of questions. What was it like to be Jesus at age two? What was it like to take His first wobbly steps onto the green grass of a world He had spoken into being? What was it like to be five or six, to lose His front teeth, to sound out words and learn how to read? What was it like to look into the countenance of any person and to see through the looking glass of their heart? Jesus knew how to read a room just like His Father. In a world perplexed by mysteries, there were no mysteries to Him. What was it like to grow up with a mother who had miraculously borne Him, a mother who comforted the One who came to comfort the world? How did it feel to be a man in His thirties, wiping tears away from the same face that had wiped away His own as a child? How did it feel to be a supernatural, unrepeatable miracle but need food to stay alive and sleep to function? Jesus lived into the dichotomy of the miraculous and the mundane. He lived into the tension of the supernatural and the natural.

He healed the sick. He also cried. He walked on water. He also knew rejection. He laughed *and* He was disappointed. He felt hunger *and* the joy of satiation. He had friends *and* no place to lay His head. Why does this matter? This matters because it has relational implications. Emmanuel—God with us—was not a concept. He was a person who lived into all the complexity of the human experience with the power of God's divinity flowing through His veins. But the nuances of His own humanity never diminished the fullness of His deity. His journey in our homesick world simply sealed His power with the authority of compassionate love.

God stooped down low in the long descent of Jesus' life to become one of us in order to have intimate, real-time friendship informed by the authority of lived experience. Jesus came to demonstrate the loving heart of the Father, and He did this in a million different human ways.

The Gospels are crystal clear about the private life and public ministry of Jesus Christ. There is no question Jesus came to do His Father's will. His life and ministry were centered on one thing: relational alignment. Nothing and no one would ever come between Him, the Father, and the Holy Spirit. Jesus walked in perfect harmony with His holy family of origin. His example of relational unity leads us to a foundational principle for those who long to live in the way of Jesus.

Consecration

Those who desire to truly follow Jesus will yield to a life of consecration. Consecration means having a life set apart for God Himself, in relationship and then in practice. It is a life that carries the fragrance of devotion that flows from a continual awareness of and interaction with God's presence and an abstinence from anything that leads away from a unified, relationship-first life with Him. A life of consecration not only makes one effective spiritually but also buffers us from the hazards of a homesick world. Do you want to know God intimately? Do you want to live in the power of the Spirit? Then there is only one path available to you, and it is the narrow road.

> [Jesus said,] "Enter by the narrow gate. For the gate is
> wide and the way is easy that leads to destruction, and
> those who enter by it are many. For the gate is narrow
> and the way is hard that leads to life, and those who find
> it are few."
> MATTHEW 7:13-14, ESV

You won't find many people on the narrow road, but human companionship isn't the goal of the invitation. You *will* find God Himself and become immersed in the warmth of His personhood, insulated from the cold, thin air of a life void of soul-level fulfillment. As you abide in the permanent home of His presence, you may be alone but not lonely. God the Father, Jesus the Son, and the Holy Spirit become the friends you've always longed for. Holy intimacy with a personal, Trinitarian God becomes the sustaining light of every new morning and every new beginning. The fullness of friendship becomes the brightest-burning star in the blackest of nights, in the cruelest of endings. God becomes the grace we need to say goodbye and thank you in the same breath. His sufficiency oxygenates our sentences and our seasons. This kind of intimacy may seem countercultural because it is. Here in the West our priority for individuality often snuffs out the smoldering wick of our hunger for God. The result is a distant, conceptual way of relating to Him (and, often, an avoidance of other sources of spiritual authority that bear His name). We know there's something missing, but we are at war with our emotional, mental, and physical urges. We are at war with surrender. We want to be the masters of our lives, the captains of our ships. Our autonomy and desire for control line the wide gate, and this approach means we will never scale the wall of intimacy to move beyond the realm of acquaintance and into deeper, real-time friendship with God. We will do just enough to check our religious boxes without coming face to face with Christ, to catch His fragrance, to spread the aroma of His love to a watching world. This posture toward God invites us to lay down our lives and exchange our systems of control for yielded lives of abiding in Him. In the words of pastor and author Tim Keller,

> When you come to Christ, you must drop your
> conditions. What does that mean? It means you have
> to give up the right to say, "I will obey you *if* . . . I will
> do this *if* . . ." As soon as you say, "I will obey you *if*,"
> that is not obedience at all. You are saying: "You are
> my adviser, not my Lord. I will be happy to take your
> recommendations. And I might even do some of them."
> No. If you want Jesus *with you*, you have to give up
> the right to self-determination. Self-denial is an act of
> rebellion against our late-modern culture of self-assertion.
> But that is what we are called to. Nothing less.[1]

Consecration resists the winds of human preference and the lure of cultural compromise and instead grounds us in covenantal loyalty to God above all else. And while one may think complete surrender to and alignment with God must have been easy for

Jesus, it is important for us to remember that His life was not void of distractions or temptations. He did not float on a cloud above the snares of humanity, nor did He bypass the tension of a post-Eden world. His desert encounter with the enemy alone proves Jesus was not above being presented with the treacherous realities of traversing our homesick world. Matthew 4:1-11 gives us an account of this truth:

> Jesus was led by the Spirit into the wilderness to be tempted by the devil. After fasting forty days and forty nights, he was hungry. The tempter came to him and said, "If you are the Son of God, tell these stones to become bread."
>
> Jesus answered, "It is written: 'Man shall not live on bread alone, but on every word that comes from the mouth of God.'"
>
> Then the devil took him to the holy city and had him stand on the highest point of the temple. "If you are the Son of God," he said, "throw yourself down. For it is written:
>
> "'He will command his angels concerning you,
> and they will lift you up in their hands,
> so that you will not strike your foot against a stone.'"
>
> Jesus answered him, "It is also written: 'Do not put the Lord your God to the test.'"
>
> Again, the devil took him to a very high mountain and showed him all the kingdoms of the world and their splendor. "All this I will give you," he said, "if you will bow down and worship me."

Jesus said to him, "Away from me, Satan! For it is written: 'Worship the Lord your God, and serve him only.'"

Then the devil left him, and angels came and attended him.

There are some things God will not save us from on this side of heaven, and it is safe to say that if Jesus was not spared from temptation, you and I will not be spared from temptation. So it is important to extract the meaning of this period of testing for those of us who long to follow the scent of surrender. The road we are called to is narrow and winding. With this said, if there is a supernatural call and a supernatural grace on a person, you can be sure there has been and will be supernatural warfare. One of the enemy's tactics is to dull our sobriety in respect to the reality of Ephesians 6:12. How will we take up arms to fight a battle we don't believe is truly being waged against us? Spiritual warfare is not reserved for a special category of believers. Every Christ follower sojourns through this world with a bull's-eye on their back, exposed to flaming arrows and invisible threats as outlined in this biblical truth:

> Our struggle is not against flesh and blood, but against the rulers, against the authorities, against the powers of this dark world and against the spiritual forces of evil in the heavenly realms.
>
> EPHESIANS 6:12

How did Jesus handle this? When led by the Holy Spirit into the desert temptation, at war with the enemy, the flesh, and the world, Jesus did three things:

- fasted,
- prayed, and
- resisted temptation.

The lure of satiation. The dare of demonstrating His authority. The promise of power, glory, and kingdoms. We as a culture have a fascination with these things. But they are not always exclusively offered by God Himself. In this passage of Scripture the enemy offers to Jesus things our culture reveres in exchange for worship and idolatry. And here's the truth—he continues to enact the same strategy in our world today.

The enemy works in exploitation and deceit, and any area of our invisible or visible lives in which we are experiencing starvation will be a prime target for a heightened level of spiritually charged warfare. The enemy will attempt to exploit our needs, vulnerabilities, weaknesses, and wounds and then present us with pseudosolutions steeped in lies and error. But Jesus passed these tests through the command of Scripture and, in so doing, the idols of humanity—the snares of the flesh, the enemy, and the world—would hold no power over Him as He entered His public ministry.

The way of Jesus acknowledges that

1. God's Word is the final authority,
2. God Himself is our Source in a world of resources,
3. oneness with God in consecration is both a calling and a discipline, and
4. we are eternal beings called to live with an eternal line of sight.

Jesus never substituted the eternal for the temporal, nor did He substitute intimacy with God for influence for Him.

This is a sharp dichotomy to the reality of our day. The way of Jesus along the narrow road means private devotion over public platform.

Jesus set His gaze in the direction of oneness with God, and out of this devotion flowed His Father's will. This would deliver Him into a both/and kind of ministry . . . into a place where He would minister to the masses through the Sermon on the Mount *and* give His life away in the obscurity of small gatherings and one-on-one encounters. He would sit with Nicodemus eye to eye. He would also stand in proximity to the woman at the well to narrate her life and offer her a seat at redemption's table.

Jesus' life was marked by

- purity,
- simplicity,
- humility, and
- submission.

These virtues flowed from Jesus and marked Him as God's beloved, in whom He was well pleased (Matthew 3:17). The purity of being fully aligned with the Father's will was met with a desire to simply receive what God the Father wanted to give Him. Jesus' humility to live in a long and lowly descent was centered in His submission to obey, no matter the cost. Jesus did not strive for earthly gain. He did not subscribe to an earning system. He did not strategize or perform. Jesus was secure in God's choice of Him and did not desire to yield to the world's systems of control and approval. This is where we can clearly see a dichotomy between the life He lived and the realities of modern-day culture.

Put an End to Striving

In our present age, life begins and ends with numbers and evaluations. Perfect attendance. SAT scores. Annual reviews. Yearly salaries. 401(k)s. And instead of being primed for the simplicity of a vertically aligned life with God, we are immersed in an ocean of numerical expectations. If we desire to live in the way of Jesus, we will have to swim upstream against the current of a cultural ideology founded on one general formula:

Performance + Achievement = Certainty

Certainty is defined as "a fact that is *definitely* true or an event that is *definitely* going to take place."[2]

Upward mobility, in all its forms, is our performance strategy of choice in the West: Do more and try harder so you can achieve. If you achieve, you can be certain you will belong, be praised, avoid rejection, sidestep lack, secure happiness, become worthy of love: at school and church, in our careers and relationships.

From our earliest moments, the pressure to perform drives us to accumulate achievements, to "earn" our worth. While none of us would argue with the necessity of work and healthy stewardship, we've all experienced the emotional, physical, mental, spiritual, and relational sting when our efforts to succeed fall short.

We are not robots. We have not been programmed. We are not machines. We are beating hearts. We are human beings. We are sons and daughters whom God dearly loves, and we are living in a post-Eden world where life is far from perfect because we have all left the Garden. So where do we turn when we experience the inevitable emptiness and disappointment that surfaces when we achieve only to realize that our version of Eden doesn't satisfy us on a soul level? We have two primary choices: We will either go deeper into our systems of control or we will reach for the way of Jesus.

When I strive for my own version of certainty and pursue my own false Edens, I essentially believe that my way, my timing, and my plan is better than Jesus'. I essentially live from the belief that I am the guiding force for my own life. But when I choose humility and surrender my life to God's way, His timing, and His plan, I yield to His sovereignty as the guiding force for the life He's entrusted me with. I believe that He is the final authority over all things.

Biblical faith has never been about human certainty. Simply recall the founding father in the family of God. Hebrews 11:8 reminds us, "By faith Abraham, when called to go to a place he would later receive as his inheritance, obeyed and went, even though he did not know where he was going."

Abraham *did not know* where he was going. His faith was rooted not in his own certainty but in God's faithfulness. Moses was not given an advance blueprint when he darkened the door of Pharaoh's quarters to announce God's commands, but he trusted in God's hand. Joseph could not see the trajectory of his future clearly in the throes of imprisonment, but he knew God was with him. David pursued God's presence as a person in obscurity without an invitation to influence. Mary surrendered her unlikeliness to become useful in God's plan to redeem the world. John the Baptist buried himself like a seed in the ground of private devotion to God without a need to make a name for himself. Peter's faith was sown in the rugged terrain of his own failure, and still he followed the risen Jesus and flourished as an appointed champion of the gospel he had once denied. Paul's divine interruption on the road to Damascus propelled him into the wild winds of the Holy Spirit's leading, but it was his friendship with God, not supernatural signs and wonders, that became the animating center of his life. The stories of every person chronicled in this book reveal that God was not and is not a means to an end, nor is He a formula to master. He is a person whose love and sovereign line of sight is our only certainty and our only true home in a homesick world.

Faith in God as a person means we cease striving in order to instead rest in an all-knowing, all-powerful, and all-present God who is in the work of bringing something beautiful to bear in our lives in every season and circumstance. It's a life founded on knowing that this beauty will not come by our own might or our own power but by the Spirit of God and our willingness to hear and know His voice.

In contrast, cultural Christianity in the West has increasingly been centered around a "kill it for the Kingdom" mentality. This phrase is brought to you by decades of church cultures that create approaches to missional activity that prioritize output (in the name of Jesus) more than intimacy with the actual person of Jesus. While "kill it for the Kingdom" varies in expression across denominations and faith communities, what does it actually mean? How is it measured? Our cultural fixation with numerical strength is often at the root of it all. The number of attendees at our events. The number of followers on our social media accounts. How many zeros are on the check that was written. The cultural idol of upward mobility finds its way into greenrooms and boardrooms and every room where there is a beating heart breathing post-Eden air. *Do we stack up as the best and the biggest in the room, on the team, in the organization, in the state?* These are the invisible questions echoing off the walls of our hearts.

To be clear, advancing the Kingdom is not the problem. Many

of the aforementioned things would not be linked to a spiritual formation issue if those developments had happened as a natural response to the activity of God because He *does* impart growth. God *does* ignite change. God plants good trees that bear good fruit. But sometimes the movements we see in our culture at large are not movements of the Spirit. How do we know this? While there are many dimensions to this conversation, one important concern surfaces when faith becomes more about the consumption of religious experiences than the transformation of hearts and lives. In the life and times of cultural Christianity, we have seen that not all that happens in the name of God and in the name of His Kingdom come originates from the Spirit of God. Scripture clearly testifies to this as well:

> [Jesus said,] "Not everyone who says to me, 'Lord, Lord,'
> will enter the kingdom of heaven, but only the one who
> does the will of my Father who is in heaven. Many will
> say to me on that day, 'Lord, Lord, did we not prophesy
> in your name and in your name drive out demons and
> in your name perform many miracles?' Then I will tell
> them plainly, 'I never knew you. Away from me, you
> evildoers!'"
> MATTHEW 7:21-23

"I never knew you" is a relational statement. This text applies to a people who went about doing things in the name of God without knowing Him intimately in the secret place of private devotion. This is indicative of those who may have been perceived as having operated in the gifts of the Spirit but who did not operate out of intimacy with the Father.

This is a time-sensitive, critical truth because an entire

generation of Christ followers have been led to believe that as long as they achieve in the name of God publicly, they are in relational good standing with Him privately. Our culture has conditioned society, en masse, to believe that being influential for God is better than being intimate with God, and we have done so to the detriment of our souls.

We are caught in a cultural vortex where striving for excellence, advancement, growth, and upward mobility are the little-*g* gods of our time. But what has this secured for us? Are our lives overflowing with the fruit of the Spirit? Do we love our enemies? Do we care about people experiencing homelessness? Do we care about the stranger? Are we witnessing true transformation take place in the lives of our attendees, our followers, our families, our children? Is there a before-and-after effect at our conferences, tours, and gatherings? How many are experiencing transformation on a soul level? How many have the power of the Spirit to place others' interests above their own and to follow in the example of Christ's narrow way? How are we doing in the wake of all the cultural pressure to perform? Is this a cross Jesus placed on our backs or a cross we bear out of our unhealed wounds or our own choosing? Do we have the peace of Christ in our hearts? Are we sleeping well at night?

We like our systems of control, and it's evident that we've come to prefer them over the wild winds of the Spirit . . . over living in the pure, simple, humble submission of learning to hear and know the Father's voice so we can walk in union with our Trinitarian God. Psychologist David Benner says:

> Fearful people live within restrictive boundaries. . . .
> . . . People who live in fear feel compelled to remain in control. They attempt to control themselves and they

attempt to control their world. Often despite their best intentions, this spills over into efforts to control others. . . .

Fear also blocks responsiveness to others. The fearful person may appear deeply loving, but fear always interferes with the impulse toward love. Energy invested in maintaining safety and comfort always depletes energy available for love of others.[3]

It's clear we are seeking more, but the more we seek is not found through the gate that is open and wide. The more we seek is only available through the narrow gate, the way of Jesus. The more we seek on a soul level is the stuff of our peace. The more we seek is His presence, on earth as it is in heaven. It is being able to hear and know His voice. In this cultural moment we are like half-fed sheep longing for the nourishment of the Great Shepherd when God Himself is holding out His merciful right hand. We've forgotten how to posture ourselves to stoop low and drink from the cup of a carpenter's son. We've lost sight of what it means to live in submission in a vertically aligned life with Him in which we slow down long enough to listen and discern what it means to simply receive what is being given from His hand.

Will You Return to Him?

God is inviting us into the great returning. He is inviting us to return to His presence and His personhood. He is calling us to cultivate spaces centered around a relationship-first approach to His Word and His Spirit, an approach that prioritizes radical loyalty to Him over human outcomes. And in so doing, He's inviting us into the purity of His presence, the pathway through which we will see His Kingdom come on earth as it is in heaven. He's calling us back into the kind of true hunger that refuses to settle for consumer-driven, conceptual, cultural Christianity and is nourished instead by nothing less than a depth of relational intimacy that transforms us into the image of Jesus.

Remember: It is not followers we are after; it is disciples. Followers are impressed. Disciples are transformed. God is inviting us to awaken to the difference as we build in His name. He is beckoning us back to fasting and prayer, age-old practices in the way of Jesus to appeal to God for a move of the Spirit that will snuff out the idols of our day and usher in His transforming presence.

But this calling is not about human effort. There has been no shortage of human effort. We write informative books. We pen killer worship songs. We see platforms with followers in the millions, and yet there is a growing sense that many people offer a public form of godliness but neglect to cultivate private connection with the true Source of transformational power, in their own secret place with God.

Having grown up in a setting where the secret place was the birthplace of the miraculous and supernatural, I feel exceptionally passionate about this invitation to return to the purity of God's presence. But I am not the first person to sense this sacred stirring. The fathers and mothers of our faith whom we have chronicled in this book illustrate what it means to live a life yielded to God and to be formed in the fires of their full yes to Him. In a culture that tells us our power is in what we have accumulated, what we have accomplished, and whom we are associated with, I pray this book has reminded you that your power is in who you trust. Your power is in who you seek in the secret place, where the private pages of your life are written and read by the Author of life and "every good and perfect gift" (James 1:17). Your power is held in the storehouse of your permanent home in Him.

Throughout the biblical narrative we see that we have been set in a relational story with a relational Father. God is not a concept. He is not an excuse to dress up on Sunday morning. He is not a conduit for a dream. He is not a missional strategy. He is a Trinitarian God made of three *persons*. In the pages of Scripture God is a person who fathers each of His children with loving intentionality. God is a person who desires to relationally care for His sons and daughters. The people of God are not expected to *earn* their title as beloved children; they are simply invited to *receive* what is being given by God the Father. In fact, this invitation into family and relational safety begins with the Trinity. God chose family. He chose relationship from the very beginning, with Jesus the Son and the Holy Spirit. In His infinite wisdom and power God could've existed alone but He chose relationship before the dawn of time. He set a holy precedent that will never be reversed. Relationship is at the very heart of God. Family is God's design, from the intimate communion of the Garden of Eden to the long table set before us in eternity. God is calling you, by name, to Himself.

I pray you have felt the glow of God's porch light calling you home to a very personal return. As you leave the experience of this book, I want to leave you with this benediction:

The wind of life is a howling mystery, but the Spirit carries us on that current into the deep places of God to hide us in His secrets. He invites us home to His friendship and the family of our origin, the familiar safety of the Holy Trinity. God Himself is light-years ahead of our human understanding. And yet He is also home. To go deeper into

Him is to go deeper into mystery and deeper into trust. Our belongingness in Him was never dependent on our ability to comprehend it. We are not just card-carrying citizens in our Father's country—we are heirs. We are native to the land and the language of love we were born into when we were fearfully and wonderfully made in our mothers' wombs. And when fear echoes out in the distance, a reverberating memory of exile, the whisper of God's love calling you back home will always be crystalline. As you return to the permanent home of His presence, He will meet you on the winds of courage to carry you into the secret place, to hear His voice, to seal you and send you out with His instruction. You may leave your understanding of safety, but you'll always be home.

Go, give light to the city on a hill that bears your name. Carry your candle, that small flicker of faith that has been lit for you. Beckon the Spirit to breathe on it until it reaches the size of the unencumbered, unrestrained, and wild ways of the love of God. Go until the dark night of your need for understanding has passed and turned into the dawn of trust, until your human requirements die a death and are swallowed in the life and light of holy influence. Look down the halls of your history, your spiritual ancestry, the stories of the fathers and mothers gone before you. They died for a faith they never fully understood in the finite reaches of their minds. And yet they won the war waged in the human heart to pass from this life to the next victorious, as the last measures of their heartbeats kept time with the great Conductor of the symphony of all things. The chorus of their faithfulness echoes out even now and into eternity. Go, fall forward and free into childlike trust once again.

Whether you turn to the right or to the left, your ears will hear a voice behind you, saying, "This is the way; walk in it."

ISAIAH 30:21

Reflection Questions

1. Jesus' life was marked by purity, simplicity, humility, and submission. Which of these areas do you sense God inviting you to grow in?

2. If Jesus was not exempt from temptation, what implications does that have for you and me? What are some ways we can protect ourselves from temptation?

3. Followers are impressed. Disciples are changed. If a tree is known by its fruit, how can we cultivate pathways, spaces, and relationships that prioritize spiritual transformation over all other outcomes?

4. Are there any decisions in your life that have been made with a priority on cultural criteria as opposed to the purity of God's Kingdom values? What does radical loyalty to God, as the final authority over all things, look like for you as you consider moving forward with a new commitment to return to Him with all your heart?

ACKNOWLEDGMENTS

Jake, Sophie, and Jonah: "You give me the sun and the moon but you're more than oceans and stars in the universe of my heart."[1]

Mom, Dad, and Marshall: There will always be a deep love and an understanding between us that requires very few words. I pray these pages have honored your sacrifice, faithfulness, and radical loyalty to God. We've lived these stories, and now the world will know.

Templo De Poder Church: Thank you for shaping the core of all I believe about God, the Bible, and the life-altering beauty possible in the body of Christ. Your relationship-first hearts, and your homemade buñuelos, have marked me for life.

Everyone from NavPress and Tyndale—for making this book possible.

Renee Farkas—for being my spiritual director and one of my safest places.

Trinity McFadden and The Bindery—for the gift of being believed in.

All my close friends—for listening to ten-minute voice memos and bearing all things with me. Thank you for staying, no matter the season.

Glen and Mary Godsey: You stand now among the great cloud of witnesses, but your example is still central to my heart. You taught us how to love and shepherd for a lifetime and to finish well. This book is as much yours as it is mine.

NOTES

INTRODUCTION | GOD IS OUR PERMANENT HOME

1. As quoted in David Horton, *The Portable Seminary: A Master's Level Overview in One Volume*, 1st ed. (Minneapolis: Bethany House, 2006), 88–89. Gordon R. Lewis, "Attributes of God," in *Evangelical Dictionary of Theology*, ed. Walter A. Elwell (Grand Rapids: Baker Academic, 2007), 492.

CHAPTER 1 | A FAMILY FOUNDED ON THE IMPOSSIBLE

1. Brennan Manning, *Ruthless Trust: The Ragamuffin's Path to God* (New York: HarperCollins, 2002).
2. Quotation shared with the author in personal conversation. Mother Teresa, as quoted in JoAnne Christie and John D. Jerome, comps., *Remembering Mother Teresa* (Manotick, Ontario: Towerhill Charity Group, 2008), 95.

CHAPTER 2 | THE UNDOING

1. Anton Ego (voiced by Peter O'Toole), *Ratatouille* (Emeryville, CA: Pixar, 2007), DVD.
2. Ruth Haley Barton, *Strengthening the Soul of Your Leadership: Seeking God in the Crucible of Ministry*, 2nd ed. (Downers Grove, IL: InterVaristy Press, 2018), 55.
3. Dallas Willard, *Hearing God: Developing a Conversational Relationship with God*, exp. ed. (Downers Grove, IL: InterVarsity Press, 2012).
4. Richard J. Foster, *Celebration of Discipline: The Path to Spiritual Growth*, 25th anniv. ed. (New York: HarperCollins, 1998), 24.
5. Peter Scazzero, *Emotionally Healthy Discipleship: Moving from Shallow Christianity to Deep Transformation* (Grand Rapids: Zondervan, 2021), chap. 3.

CHAPTER 4 | HEART OPEN, WALLS DOWN

1. Paul David Tripp, *Awe: Why It Matters for Everything We Think, Say, and Do* (Wheaton, IL: Crossway, 2015), chap. 5.
2. Dan B. Allender, in "Engaging Our Story of Harm and Abuse," *The Allender Center Podcast*, December 2014, https://open.spotify.com /episode/2ys5yIn2dZz5ExGBOFfTYr.
3. Richard Plass and James Cofield, *The Relational Soul: Moving from False Self to Deep Connection* (Downers Grove, IL: InterVarsity Press, 2014), 83.
4. Jeremy Benson and Newt Likier, "How Many Galaxies Are in the Universe?" *The Sound of Science*, Norhern Public Radio, March 11, 2022, https://www.northernpublicradio.org/2022-03-11/the-sound -of-science-how-many-galaxies-are-in-the-universe.

CHAPTER 5 | THE FREEDOM OF SURRENDER

1. Thomas Merton, *Thoughts in Solitude* (New York: Farrar, Straus and Giroux, 1999), 23.
2. Rich Mullins, "The Love of God," *Never Picture Perfect* © 1989 Reunion Records.
3. Written and composed by Pete Seeger. Popularized by The Byrds, "Turn! Turn! Turn! (To Everything There Is a Season)," *Turn! Turn! Turn!* © 1965 Columbia.

CHAPTER 6 | THE SECRET PLACE

1. R. C. H. Lenski, *The Interpretation of St. Luke's Gospel 1–11* (Minneapolis: Augsburg Fortress, 1946), 176.
2. Dallas Willard, *The Divine Conspiracy: Rediscovering Our Hidden Life in God* (San Francisco: HarperCollins, 1998), 355.
3. Henri J. M. Nouwen, *In the Name of Jesus: Reflections on Christian Leadership* (New York: Crossroad, 1989), 35.
4. Alistair Begg, "The Preacher John the Baptist (Part 1 of 2) - 10/07/22," *Truth for Life*, YouTube video, 24:59, accessed May 21, 2024, https:// www.youtube.com/watch?v=fYuZSNO0MhQ&t=136s.

CHAPTER 7 | FAILING FORWARD

1. Dallas Willard, *Renovation of the Heart: Putting On the Character of Christ*, 20th anniv. ed. (Colorado Springs: NavPress, 2021), 24–25.
2. Dan B. Allender, *Leading with a Limp: Take Full Advantage of Your Most Powerful Weakness* (Colorado Springs: WaterBrook, 2008), 70.
3. I heard this quote live when I took a trip to Redding, California, in 2018. Jason Upton, "The Stirring Messages: 2—Finding God and

Ourselves," July 1, 2018, https://podcasts.apple.com/us/podcast/2
-finding-god-and-ourselves/id555991101?i=1000415660482.

4. Pete Scazzero, *Emotionally Healthy Spirituality: It's Impossible to Be
Spiritually Mature While Remaining Emotionally Immature* (Grand
Rapids: Zondervan, 2017), 147.

CHAPTER 8 | THE TOMB IS A WOMB

1. One of my mentors gave me this phrase in my early twenties. I believe
it was his own paraphrase of a chapter in Frederick Buechner's book
Wishful Thinking: A Seeker's ABC (San Francisco: HarperCollins,
1993).

2. Frederick Buechner, quoted in Melissa Maimone, *The Radiant
Midnight: Depression, Grace, and the Gifts of a Dark Place* (Eugene,
OR: Harvest House, 2019), 213.

3. Paul is traditionally credited with writing thirteen Bible books.

CHAPTER 9 | THE RETURNING

1. Timothy Keller, *Hidden Christmas: The Surprising Truth Behind the
Birth of Christ* (New York: Penguin, 2018), 58.

2. *Oxford Pocket Dictionary of Current English*, s.v. "certainty (*n.*),"
accessed June 13, 2024, https://www.encyclopedia.com/medicine
/psychology/psychology-and-psychiatry/certainty. Emphasis added.

3. David G. Benner, *Surrender to Love: Discovering the Heart of Christian
Spirituality*, exp. ed. (Downers Grove, IL: InterVarsity Press, 2015),
41–42.

ACKNOWLEDGMENTS

1. Tanya Godsey, "The Universe of My Heart" © 2023.

NavPress is the book-publishing arm of The Navigators.

Since 1933, The Navigators has helped people around the world bring hope and purpose to others in college campuses, local churches, workplaces, neighborhoods, and hard-to-reach places all over the world, face-to-face and person-by-person in an approach we call Life-to-Life® discipleship. We have committed together to know Christ, make Him known, and help others do the same.®

Would you like to join this adventure of discipleship and disciplemaking?

- Take a Digital Discipleship Journey at **navigators.org/disciplemaking**.
- Get more discipleship and disciplemaking content at **thedisciplemaker.org**.
- Find your next book, Bible, or discipleship resource at **navpress.com**.

 @NavPressPublishing

 @NavPress

 @navpressbooks

CP1790